AFTER THE LAST PR

SECOND EDITION

Cover and formatting by
Dave Zobel
dzobel Illustration

2018 by

Flying Feet Running Programs, LLC

Westminster, MD

dpgflyingfeet@gmail.com

Printed and bound in the United States of America

First Edition 2010

Second Edition 2018

WITH GRATITUDE
TO ALL THOSE
WHO HAVE RUN
BESIDE ME.

TABLE OF CONTENTS

PREFACE

I'm a runner deep down in the core of my person, and I think I've earned the right to say that. In many respects, the words on these pages have documented the experiences that have made me who I am, not just as a runner, but as a person too. My running and my life are forever intertwined.

I would dare to say that every positive quality I possess has either been formed or strengthened through running. If not for running, I would be but a fraction of who I am today. I know that sounds far reaching and maybe you can't understand, but it is true nonetheless.

And, as much as running has contributed to my success, even more, it has enhanced my well being. That's not something I sought to gain from running, it just happened.

Imagine the sense of accomplishment you might feel by making time in the day to do something good for yourself – something that most people aren't willing to do. Imagine how you might feel if you did that everyday for a week, and then for a month. Imagine if you did that for as long as you could remember. How would that make you feel about yourself?

And on the most difficult days, when it was cold, or hot, when it was windy and rainy, what if you didn't make excuses? And, when something was pulling your attention elsewhere, and it would be easy to let yourself off the hook, what if you didn't? How would that impact your ability to deal with adversity?

Running has taught me that the relief that comes from taking the easy road is short lived, but that the rewards that come from challenging yourself endure. It's taught me that the pleasure of a gift is fleeting, but that satisfaction earned is lasting.

I'm not sure most people understand that. The world is full of short cuts and handouts. Assigning responsibility to someone else is commonplace. And yet, when it comes to your own happiness and contentment, delegating is not an option. You've got to find that for yourself.

Of course, I find joy in many things, like the people I love, but nothing else in my life could ever be as good if I wasn't happy with myself. And, for me, nothing has enhanced my self-worth quite like running.

This book is about more than running; it's about valuable lessons that running teaches. It's about principles that, when applied consistently, can guide a person toward success.

The book is organized so that it progresses through a series of virtues. Each virtue is unique, and yet you will discover that they are also interconnected. Growth in one way often leads to growth in another.

Life can seem complicated, but it doesn't have to be that way. It can be as simple as taking a step in the right direction, finding a path to run on, and then paying attention to the truth and the wisdom that comes along.

And, whether you run or not, if you think that what I've learned while I was running can help you find your own way, by all means, keep reading.

INTRODUCTION: AFTER THE LAST PR

I ran my last personal record (PR) in 1989 at the age of 28. From 1982 to 1989 I raced various distances, from 5K to the marathon, and in that period I ran all my best times. Back then, running was simple. I ran to race fast, and that was pretty much it.

Since then, I haven't come close to beating any of those PRs. So why, you might wonder, am I still running almost thirty years later?

I could give you simple reasons. Running boosts my confidence. It keeps me fit. I enjoy being around other runners. But the real reason is far more complicated than any of those things.

Each time I run, the unwelcome noises of life quiet. The thick pressure of work subsides. In the simple rhythm of running, I return to my core.

It's there, at my center, where I remember why I'm here. It's there that I remember what I love. There reside the principles and values that guide me. Life pulls me away from all that. Running moves me back.

I can begin a run faced with a complicated dilemma and finish it with clear vision. Every conflict that's thrown my way is resolved when I remember what's important, and running never fails to remind me what that is.

There's more. Running challenges me. A thousand times, it's confronted me with obstacles I didn't think I'd overcome. It's brought fatigue and weariness, and yet even in the throes of exhaustion, it leaves a small burning ember of strength, always just enough. After so many trials, I've learned that hope is always present if you look hard enough, and hope is a precious thing.

I still remember all my fastest races. I remember the toil in the training, the anticipation of the starting lines and the strategy of competition. I can still feel the exhilaration of those finish lines, knowing I'd surpassed my best yet again and wondering where the next plateau would lead me.

When I was running those races, my single motivation was competition, reaching ever higher levels of success. I'm thankful that I had running to feed my competitive spirit, but even more thankful that my competitive spirit led me to running.

I didn't realize it at the time, but searching for my potential as a runner taught me how to find my potential as a person. In the process of trying to do my best, I learned how to be my best. Running formed my core values, and my core values shape my life.

I'm much slower than I used to be, but that's okay. It's not as much about speed anymore. There's something more important to me – living virtuously.

When it comes to that, I know I still have some unused potential, but each run seems to move me a little bit closer. And that's why I'm still running, so long after my last PR.

CHAPTER 1:

FAITH
TRUSTING IN A SET OF BELIEFS

———————•◄———————

I was searching through a stack of my old running photographs looking for a spark of inspiration. There are hundreds of memories and stories hidden there, and they seldom fail to rouse an idea.

The pictures span a period of many years, but most of the races are still fixed in my mind, just as the images are fixed on the paper.

There is one from my very first marathon. My stride is choppy, weighted down with the pain of distance and discouraged pride. I hadn't prepared well, somehow believing that ability alone would be enough. When reality struck, still many miles from the finish line, all I could do was rely on the mercy of knowing that each step was one closer to the end.

I was searching through a stack of my old running photographs looking for a spark of inspiration. There are hundreds of memories and stories hidden there, and they seldom fail to rouse an idea.

The pictures span a period of many years, but most of the races are still fixed in my mind, just as the images are fixed on the paper.

There is one from my very first marathon. My stride is choppy, weighted down with the pain of distance and discouraged pride. I hadn't prepared well, somehow believing that ability alone would be enough. When reality struck, still many miles from the finish line, all I could do was rely on the mercy of knowing that each step was one closer to the end.

Another picture, taken about seven years after the first one, shows a different posture. There is confidence in my expression and concentration in my eyes. My stride is wide and strong as I pull away from the competitors who had tried desperately to stay on my shoulder.

If you looked through the pictures yourself, you would see a parade of images. In the beginning, a boy finds joy as he discovers himself. Slowly, the years become evident as a seasoned competitor emerges. And then, in more recent photographs, a man still tries to find success doing what he loves.

The pictures seem to tell of a seamless journey, like a life that has followed a well-planned course, but that's not the case. There have been starts and stops. There were moments of choice, sometimes understood and sometimes not, that could have changed everything.

I've been the benefactor of good fortune. Blessed with a touch of ability, I stumbled upon running as I searched for identity in my youth. It was only through trial and error that I ultimately found success, and while I know I fell far short of my potential, it is difficult now to feel anything less than satisfied. Running, after all, has shaped me.

The truth is, though, that something more than luck lies at the center of my story. And while I'll never argue that good fortune has played a part in my success, it seems appropriate to give the credit to something much more meaningful.

Faith is the thread that held the pieces of my running journey together. It gave me hope when I was in the throes of exhaustion. It let me believe in myself when I was on the verge of something great. Faith added meaning to victory and gave purpose to defeat. It even provided assurance when, for one reason or another, I had to put running aside for a time.

Faith helps us believe what our simple minds can't comprehend. Without it, greatness can fade to ordinary or worse. But with it, a disjointed journey can become spectacular, just like mine.

Sometimes, the pace of change startles me, and as I parked the car for a run, I couldn't help but think about the news on the radio. It wasn't long ago that we were hearing words like "stability" and "prosperity" and suddenly there was a crisis to deal with.

In times like these, I need something firm to hold onto. Ever since I can remember, running has provided that. When life has brought me sadness or heartache, hardship or insecurity, running has always given me a foundation of security. On this particular day, I needed just a little something more, so I drove to an old fire trail that I remembered from years ago.

The trail is surrounded by miles of wooded acres, and as my run found a tempo, I tried to recall the things I was about to pass. When I was younger I lived close by, and the trail had been a frequent training route.

Even before then, as a boy, I shared the trail with my grandfather. We would walk until we arrived at the lake and then we'd search for beavers along the shoreline. I passed the spot where we would find trees lying along the pathway, casualties of the beavers' work.

As I ran, the sun danced on the water, and I stopped worrying about the news on the radio. Instead, I began thinking about how much time had passed since I'd last moved past that water. In the years since, I had met my wife, and we had started a family. We worked hard to build a life, make a home, and raise our kids. Now, they are young adults and on their own personal journeys toward independence.

With several miles behind me, I remembered a place where I used to stop and stretch. I started looking for it as the path curved along the water.

When I reached the spot I was looking for, I stopped and walked down to the edge. There, a large rock stood against a quiet cove. I climbed onto it and listened to my breathing settle down.

The place was exactly as I remembered it. The full trees formed a barrier on the opposite side of the lake, as if to say, "There's enough beauty right here in front of you. No need to look any further." A breeze rippled the surface, and fish played in the deep water under the rock.

For a few moments, it was like no time had passed at all; I was still twenty years old and seeing it all for the very first time. It felt good to stay there for a while.

There was something different about the run back. I was surrounded by stability; it seemed like the path had been untouched since I left it. Being there helped me realize that, despite the passing years and the events surrounding me, I was mostly unchanged myself, much like the aged trees that I ran past. Something about that restored my faith and made me ready for whatever the news would be on the drive back home.

Just before the run was over, as I was about to turn away from the lake, I saw beavers swimming near the shoreline.

Scott Absher was taking a familiar run in unfamiliar territory. As he ran on the roads around his home in Maryland, his father lay dying in North Carolina. He was trying to figure out how he and his family could get there to say goodbye.

Nine months before, Scott's dad had become ill unexpectedly. There was a surgery, which later seemed unnecessary, and the procedure led to more serious problems. His father was left hospitalized with a feeding tube, fighting for his life.

As Scott ran through his neighborhood, he thought about the past. He realized that it was his father who had taught him that family comes first, and that hard work always pays off. His father was a caring, giving man, and he wasn't afraid to let his children know him as a person.

Scott had been running for seven years before his dad became ill. Running gave him the opportunity to stay fit within the confines of his life. He woke up early to run while everyone else was still sleeping.

His competitive nature got him started, but as he became a more experienced runner, it was the escape from daily stress that kept him running. And, as he struggled to deal with his father's failing health, that daily tranquility became even more important.

He had traveled to North Carolina regularly, watching his father fight courageously, but the challenges mounted. As the months passed by, the recurring infections took their toll, and his father needed a ventilator to cling to life.

Through all of that, it was running that helped Scott keep a sense of control. He continued his weekly schedule of running regardless of where he was. It helped him slow the world down, if only briefly, so he could deal with the enduring crisis.

As he turned onto his street to finish his run, he knew that this was the end. The doctors had told him that all hope was gone, and his father was simply waiting for the ventilator to be removed.

When Scott stopped at his driveway, there must have been a part of him that wanted to keep running. He must have felt that as long as he did, he wouldn't have to face what was coming.

When he arrived at the hospital in North Carolina, his dad was alive but unaware that his family was gathered beside him. Within an hour, he passed away.

On the day of the funeral, Scott ran up to the park in the Carolina town where he grew up. Many years ago, his father had been a member of the city council that was responsible for building the park. As he ran there, he felt an overwhelming peace, as if his dad was reassuring him – the suffering is over.

Life is always changing. Sometimes we're ready. Sometimes we're not. Either way, those of us who run understand: there is a firm connection between what we gain through running and what we need in life – a foundation of strength and a pathway to peace. As life returns to normal, Scott still has both.

This essay isn't anything like what I expected it to be. I selected several topics and tried to get started on each one of them. Nothing flowed. I'd get a few sentences out and then – nothing.

All the while, I had been thinking about my daughter's approaching birthday.

Whenever I remember the day she was born, I think about standing in the hallway of the hospital all by myself. Moments before, we were in the midst of excitement and joy when the monitor told the doctors that her heart rate had dropped dramatically.

Before I realized what was happening, they had rushed my wife into the operating room, leaving me alone. As I stood in that hallway, it was my faith that held me together. Somehow, I trusted that she would be okay.

When a nurse came out of the operating room, she saw me and pulled me inside. I walked in just in time to see the doctor lift my daughter into the world, and a few moments later she was in my arms.

As I walked her toward the hospital nursery, I didn't realize how much she would be like me. Her willful nature and her competitive spirit are mirror images of mine. And, I didn't know that she would share my passion for running.

When we first started running together, my son, who is a couple years younger, was anxious to run, too. I was cautious about having him start too soon, but in time he would join us. In a lifetime of unforgettable running memories, those runs with my kids rise above all the others.

Both of my children would follow in my running footsteps, but for my son, it was more of an activity than a sport. So, when he gave up spring track to try out for the high school play, I was happy to see him discover something he could feel more passionate about.

As a father, there have been many lessons I've tried to teach. I had a list of knowledge and experiences I wanted to transfer, but I'm afraid I've only been marginally successful. Life seems to teach better than I do.

There is something valuable, though, that I think my kids have gained from me: life is sweeter when you discover your passion and then live it faithfully.

Recently, I watched my son on the stage. He was charismatic and energetic. He was playful and engaging. He was brave and inspiring. In the words of a runner, he ran the perfect race.

Reflection is a valuable thing, isn't it? You see things differently when those things are behind you. And, experience gives you the blessing of foresight. I wish I could transfer that to my kids, but they'll have to learn about life the same way everyone else does – by living it.

On the other hand, foresight might be overrated. After all, I didn't even know what path these words would follow until I let my heart carry my fingers across the keyboard. And, if my kids can lead their lives in a similar way, I have a feeling they'll be just fine.

CHAPTER 2:

CONFIDENCE
BELIEVING IN ONE'S SELF

———————————◆ ◆———————————

I was afraid on my first day of track practice, inhibited by all the normal fears of a 14-year old boy.

Shy by nature, I preferred to stand in the background rather than get anywhere near the spotlight. I cowered away from dominant personalities, feeling more comfortable around those more like myself.

I can't tell you when I began to silence the whispers of apprehension. I imagine they began to fade in hard workouts and grow quieter still when I raced well. It was a process, not an event, as I gradually recognized that it was better to not be afraid.

By the time I was a high school senior, I finally had the courage to challenge the best runners in the state. I would hold on to the leader, determined to be recognized as a threat. Sometimes they pulled away in the final lap. Sometimes they didn't pull away.

I remember running the mile against a runner who, at the time, was the best cross-country runner in the state. I ran just off his shoulder until we entered the final turn. Then, he started an early kick, putting several meters between us.

I don't know how fast we were running as we moved passed the cheering bleachers, but it was a dead sprint for both of us. I pulled up beside him just as we approached the finish, and I felt him break as I inched ahead.

A picture in the newspaper captured the moment. My arms were raised and my mouth was wide with a conquering scream. I know now, that was the moment my fear was gone.

At the time, I didn't realize how many people live with fear, but I do now. I don't mean the terror of a Hollywood thriller; I mean the more debilitating things we fear like failure, uncertainty, and change.

Almost everyone who joins my Flying Feet group is afraid at first, in one way or another. To some degree, it's a matter of perception about the group, but it has more to do with the self-perception of the newcomer.

It is our misconceptions, I think, that are our own worst enemy. Flying Feet is made up of people who are friendly and widely diverse when it comes to their running paces. It doesn't take long to calm the concern about the group, but removing the self-doubt takes much longer.

Fear will steal your confidence and confine your dreams, and here's what you need to know about it: it is almost always self-imposed.

Running won't give you courage; it simply helps you find the courage that's always been there. It will awaken the gagged voice inside you, so that you'll finally be able to hear it say, "You can do this. You are worthy and strong."

Fear must be conquered in your most vulnerable moments, and that can be hard. But cower, and you'll suppress your greatest blessings, and that's even scarier.

Sam's wife had sent him for a few things at the grocery store, and he drove there trying to remember the brands she wanted. After he parked the car, he gulped down his last few ounces of Gatorade, wishing he had brought a second bottle along.

He noticed that the woman coming out of the store was watching curiously as he struggled to step up onto the curb. He smiled at her as she passed, owning the stiff ache from the morning run like a sign of honor.

Earlier, when the alarm had gone off at six, he resisted only briefly until he gained enough consciousness to realize he didn't have to go to work. He was out the door after downing a banana and some juice, leaving everyone else in the house still sleeping.

He had come to enjoy his Saturday morning runs more than any of the others. He felt a sense of satisfaction knowing he was accomplishing something when everyone else had yet to start their day.

He was going long this morning - twelve miles - and it would be the final long run before a half-marathon two weeks away. It was still hard to believe he was going to do it, when just a year before he couldn't run to the end of his street without walking.

Early in the run, the miles passed easily, and he spent much of the time watching the sun climb through various stages of dawn. It was only in the last few miles that he began to feel challenged. On the long runs, there was always a point when he wondered whether or not he could make it back home. He always did.

As he rounded the last turn and ran towards his house, a neighbor ventured out for the newspaper, first cup of coffee in hand. The neighbor said something like, "wish I had the time for such things," the irony apparently escaping him.

When he stopped running, the stiffness struck immediately, and he walked slowly up and down his driveway until he felt the steadiness return.

His wife had just made it to the breakfast table as he walked inside. She shook her head, still not understanding why he put himself through it all.

He didn't usually know how to explain it, but the words came more easily this particular morning. "I've spent most of my life," he told her, "trying to avoid a challenge. I've always steered clear of anything outside my comfort zone, but I'm not going to do that anymore. Running has taught me that I'm capable of more than I thought I was."

She asked him if he was capable of going to the store for a few things. Then, she kissed him, smiled, and said something he hadn't heard very often – "I'm proud of you."

He searched the aisles for the things she wanted, and even remembered all the brands. Then, he left the store grimacing as he stepped off the curb, carrying everything he needed, and then some.

I remember a May race many years ago. It was a day when a lot of good things were coming together for me. I was beginning to understand how the specifics of my training translated into race results, and I was applying what I knew in workouts. And, on this particular day with clear air and cool temperatures, I had chosen a race with just the right competition.

I was pulled through the first mile on the shoulder of a faster runner, and as we entered a downhill stretch we were flying. I felt smooth; the long, hard intervals on the track were paying off.

When things go perfectly in a race, there is little conscious thought. Thinking invites doubt and forces you to take an inventory of pain. It's to be avoided. In its place is concentration, a firm focus on the task at hand. For me, in this race, my single focus was holding on, and it resulted in the fastest 5,000-meters I had ever run.

I should have been ecstatic. Celebration should have been in order, but there was a problem. I was running a 10,000-meter race.

In a lifetime, there are moments that change life's course, whether subtly or with significance. For me, this was one of those moments. I could have decided that a 5K PR was enough and that jogging in the rest of the way was fine. I didn't do that.

The course turned onto a loop in a quiet park. There was no one there to watch us; it was only the two of us, racing along the rolling road. I clung to his shoulder, refusing to let go and knowing, if I did, I would be left to watch him pull away.

I'm not sure I can describe the emotion I was feeling. It was almost like anger, but perhaps better described as intense determination.

We left the park and headed back towards the finish following the same road we had come out on. Many runners had yet to enter the park, and they cheered as we passed them, but their voices sounded far away, muffled by the concentration.

The last couple of miles were all out. I was just holding on, so as he surged near the finish, he pulled away to win by a few strides. I finished just behind him with a huge personal best.

We all have a comfort zone, a safe room we usually avoid leaving, afraid of what might happen if we do. With preparation, we can expand its walls, but even then, our greatest potential never resides there.

That race taught me that my comfort zone is as much a confinement as it is a safe-haven. Leaving it that day made me realize that I'm capable of more than I believed. That simple understanding has stayed with me, giving me confidence whenever I've needed it, at least a thousand times since.

It had been the topic of conversation all week – there was a snowstorm coming for the weekend. Knowing I'd never get my long run in once the storm kicked in, I decided to get it done on Friday within hours of when the storm was supposed to start.

I picked a quiet route where I knew there wouldn't be much traffic and started out slowly. Now that I'm older, it takes a mile or so for my body to remember I'm a runner. I used to fight that, didn't think a serious runner should plod along, but now I find it easier to treat my body like a partner rather than a subordinate. Before long, I was moving along in the normal rhythm.

The scene around me was nothing like you would have found in the grocery store that day. The world seemed at peace with whatever was coming. There were no leaves on the trees to hide the snow that lingered from the last storm, and I could see the full beauty of the landscape around me. I'm thankful I've never retreated to a treadmill when winter comes. Solitude is better when experienced in the midst of something bigger than you.

I pressed a little harder in the second half, remembering the benefit I was hoping to get from the run, but still feeling comfortable in the effort. As I moved along a winding dirt road, the first flakes began to fall, and I knew I was one of the first to see the start of it. Within a few moments, the snow became steady, and I ran the last couple of miles in winter wonder.

When I got back home, I carried the peace with me. I don't know exactly how to describe it; I was simply ready to let myself get snowed in.

As I was waking up the next day, the news stations spoke of the epic storm. The snow was already piled up outside, still falling fast and blowing. Everyone else, like me, could do nothing but watch.

Usually, what's happening around us is beyond our control. Why then do we overreact, acting like we couldn't survive a day without milk and forgetting that melted snow makes water?

The truth is the only real control we have is self-control. By believing in our own resilience and resourcefulness, the storms around us become less important.

The next great snowstorm came just days after the first one. It was an unprecedented event, and I couldn't resist the urge to run in it. I found a plowed path to follow and suddenly turned my focus away from what was raging around me and toward my ability to get through it.

There will always be storms. Challenges are abundant. Life is better when we accept that, stop wishing them away and start believing in ourselves. After all, something on the horizon is coming either way.

In the final miles of the first Bachman Valley Half Marathon, I caught up to Scott Douglas and we ran together to share the 1983 win. After coming back to win the race outright in '84 and '87, I came to the 1988 race with a feeling of confidence.

The course had hills in places where you didn't want them, but I knew those hills well. I had trained on the course hundreds of times with some of the same runners gathered at the starting line. Our sweat was sprinkled between the gravel of the roads. Looking back, the entire fall morning gave me a comfortable feeling of familiarity. Then the race started.

The early pack quickly dwindled to two of us, and I didn't know the man on my shoulder. When you are competitors in a race, you don't share much about yourself, so as he lingered a half stride off my pace, I felt like he was trying to hide himself.

Wanting to get back into familiar territory, I surged just after the fourth mile. I felt smooth as I ran under the trees of an old dirt road. The cool air on my face told me I was running well, and I passed the five-mile mark realizing I had covered that mile in less than five minutes. It was one of the finest miles I had ever run in a race of that distance, but there was a problem. He was still there.

It was at that point in the race when my confidence crumbled. Suddenly, I was running defensively and doubting my ability to keep up. I had to convince myself at each mile marker that I could stay with him until the next one. In the eleventh mile, I lost the mental battle, and he put a gap between us that held until the end of the race. In a time faster than any of my winning times, I would finish second.

In a brief conversation afterwards, I learned that my competitor was Steven Clark. Clark had just finished a successful college running career but had never raced longer than 10,000 meters. He had spent the entire race questioning his ability to cover the half-marathon distance. It was only recently that I understood the irony in that.

It is funny how life teaches lessons in its own time. I guess that has less to do with what we're capable of understanding and more to do with what we're willing to accept. Either way, I find myself wondering how well I could have run that day if I had simply believed in myself for the entire 13.1 miles.

Each year, runners return to the hills of the Bachman Valley Half Marathon. On the course, lessons are taught but sometimes not understood until many years later.

So, I'll keep reflecting on the races of my past. I'll keep remembering the victories and the disappointments. And, sometimes, new light will be shed on something that used to be unclear, and new hope will grow from the sweat that still stains the old gravel.

CHAPTER 3:

FORTITUDE

STRENGTH OF MIND THAT ENABLES ONE TO ENDURE ADVERSITY

These words didn't come easily, but reluctantly, as if they didn't want to be heard. The thoughts and feelings formed a bottleneck, refusing to flow.

To start with, it was a week I had been dreading at work. I had to deliver difficult news and watch the emotional aftermath. Leadership has its drawbacks and leaves you standing alone sometimes.

As the week went on, I learned that several friends were dealing with loss. In one case, death had come just in time, almost mercifully. In another case it came far too swiftly, taking us by surprise. Afterwards, regardless of the details, loved ones grieved and wrestled with the unthinkable challenge of moving forward.

Others close to me were simply struggling with life itself, something we all do from time to time. The abundance of sadness was unusual, as if sorrow was suddenly contagious.

Mixed in was the constant din of bad news and propaganda, media-driven noise that has led me to be far more cynical than I ever wanted to be. And it was all just too much. So, I turned to the stone foundation that has always kept me standing before.

There was no physical purpose for the run; I wasn't looking for a workout. So, as the stiffness lingered longer than usual, I simply ignored it. I didn't have the energy to run faster anyway.

I followed my normal route, not even thinking about where I was going. In fact, thought was absent; I was unconsciously going through the run, until movement on the trail ahead caught my attention. It was a young buck, his antlers just forming behind the ears that hadn't heard me approaching. He was slowly moving toward a wide stream, and I stopped so he wouldn't notice me.

He took a drink as a breeze freed some yellow leaves that danced to the ground around him. Then I was suddenly aware of the whole striking scene: the colors, the tranquility, and him standing in the middle, a body of growing strength. I didn't want to disturb it, didn't want the picture to change, so I turned around and headed back the other way.

Sometimes I get stuck in a figurative place and can't find my way out until running leads me in a better direction. Whenever life turns ugly, running presents something beautiful. Whenever I feel weak, it gives me strength. I really don't know what I've done to deserve such a gift, but I'll accept it with gratitude.

When my run was over, nothing had changed, with the exception of my frame of mind, but that was enough to remove the bottleneck of thoughts and feelings and allow these words to form. Sometimes, trying to control life is a futile task, but I'm determined not to let it control me. And when it begins to take hold, I know exactly what to do.

The clock beside the finish line was relentless, ticking along as Lori desperately tried to reach it in less than thirty minutes. It was a goal she had shared with me and the group that was waiting for her as she struggled in the final mile of the 5K race.

Her friend Stephanie got her to start running. That's not unusual. Many people try running for the first time after being encouraged by a friend. After all, it takes courage to start as an adult, but this encouragement came in an unusual way.

Lori met Stephanie at her work, and within months they were best friends. At the time, both of them were struggling with the normal stresses of work and life, and a close friend added a foundation of comfort.

Stephanie was younger than Lori by about ten years, but that didn't seem to matter. She was smart and quick-witted, one of the funniest people Lori had ever known. Since both of their husbands were away during the evenings, they would go to Lori's house after work. Stephanie became part of Lori's family.

Over time, Lori learned about Stephanie's illness, juvenile diabetes. Stephanie had been on an insulin pump for years but didn't really take the disease seriously enough. When she developed an infection, she simply removed the pump and began using injections.

The details aren't really important. One day, Stephanie became shaky and disoriented. The next day, she was in a coma. Then she was dead. Stephanie was 30 years old. She never ran.

For a while, Lori's world was empty. The part that Stephanie had filled was vacant until Lori learned about a diabetes 5K taking place that October.

Running was hard, but Lori found purpose in preparing for the race in Stephanie's honor. Early on, she had to get beyond her self-consciousness, but that didn't take long. Running soon became a new way to cope with life's hard issues.

Three years after Stephanie's death, we waited for Lori at another finish line, the clock still moving toward thirty minutes. When we finally saw her in the distance, we weren't sure she would make it. She was pressing hard, but the seconds were ticking away. We screamed encouragement as she got closer.

Life takes its twists and turns. Sometimes we dream about what lies ahead and our dream comes true. Other times, we're unprepared. Whatever the case may be, life isn't so much about what lies around the next bend. It is about how we respond to what we find there. Lori met her goal with thirteen seconds to spare.

Time is relentless, like a clock at the finish line. If we knew what lies ahead, most of us would be more proactive. We'd take control of life. We'd do first things first and get beyond excuses.

Therein lies another secret that a running life unveils. Each day is an opportunity to find peace and clarity, and Lori finds that as she runs along, always remembering the friend who got her started.

I was hurting, but no more than the other runners in the lead pack.

We had been climbing for nearly half a mile, about 200 meters from reaching the turnaround of a four-mile race. The course was merciless, mostly downhill for the first mile and uphill for the second, and then reversed on the way back. The pack was bunched around me, all holding on and needing the relief that would come at the turnaround.

It was my final race of 1984, and I was finishing a breakout year, running several races that were perhaps the best I've ever run. My running log still has a note on the inside cover showing the goals I started the year with: 32:15 for 10K and 54:00 for ten miles. I had met one and came within seconds of the other.

When I look at that running log today, I wonder how I managed the mileage and the workouts. I long to feel the fluid motion I remember, as one run reinforced the next.

I was hurting on that hill, but I knew I had less pure speed than some of the other runners in the lead pack. On the downhill, they might use it to pull away, so I did the very opposite of what my body wanted me to do.

I sprinted, using the rest of the climb to put distance between us, and by the time I turned around they were scattered behind me, still struggling to reach the crest. They all looked at me with desperate stares, and I knew the race was already mine.

The adrenalin high on the decent was magnificent. The pain was gone. All I felt was freedom, as my legs moved on instinct. Near the base of the hill, I heard the footsteps of another runner, and he caught me briefly, but he had labored too hard to catch up. He was gone as soon as we began to climb, and I raced alone for the rest of the glorious way.

I know many would say that I'm lucky to have had the opportunity to win races, and I have to agree. In another respect, though, winning that race wasn't a gift; it was a return on investment.

Great opportunity doesn't present itself often. Sometimes, when it does, it will pass by untouched or even unrecognized. It is only with preparation that we can grasp a fleeting chance and turn it into something great.

Running is a proving ground, a place where limits are tested, and capabilities are discovered. Through running, principles are learned that can be applied both on race day, and more importantly, in life.

That's true for every runner, regardless of ability, because speed is a relative thing, but moral fiber isn't.

Some say that life has defining moments, but I think that's a misnomer. We are defined by the decisions we make, the work ethic we employ, and the discipline we display in the years before the moment happens.

We huddled together, gesturing to the camera that we were number one. The cold, damp air didn't seem to bother us. Elation has a way of warming you.

We had just won the tri-state track and field championships by a margin that caused the reporter to use the headline "Blow Out City." To say we were proud would be an understatement.

I wonder if I would recognize many of the faces if I saw them now. The years that have passed since the picture was taken have changed us, I'm sure. I wonder too if the rest of them remember that night, one I'll never forget.

When we arrived on the bus, the cold, steady rain had put my teammates in a lazy mood. Most of them were wishing the track meet would be canceled. I stood up and voiced my anger. "Let the rest of the teams worry about the weather," I said. "Then, it will be to our advantage." As a senior, I didn't have many races left, and I had a lot yet to accomplish.

By the time I stood at the starting line for the mile that night, the rain had slowed to a drizzle. I was seeded third, behind two legendary runners. One, Kelly Long, had won the 4A cross country title the previous fall. The other, Jeff Scuffins, had dominated the track that season, and he would later win the Marine Corps Marathon in a course record time of 2:14:01. That record still stands.

The race went by in a muffled blur; I was aware only that I was on Scuffins' shoulder, running just off his pace. Each lap, the starter held up fingers to show how far we had yet to run. I paid little attention, trying only to hold on.

I don't remember much about the final lap, except that Scuffins began to pull away. I never once saw Long, who would finish third. I crossed the line between the two of them, propelling myself to a new status.

I've often wondered why I ran so well that night. Maybe I felt like I had to set the tone for my teammates. Maybe it was the urgency applied by my dwindling time in high school. Perhaps it was some combination of the two. All I know for sure is that I had never been so focused. I didn't think at all. I just raced.

Too often, we all think too much. Between the day we are first told that we can accomplish anything we put our minds to and the day we realize that isn't so, we become subject to the most severe of all limitations – self-doubt.

If that's true for you, let me ask you to use your imagination for a moment. Imagine that you and I are teammates. Together, we're waiting on a bus, while a cold, hard rain beats loudly on the roof.

Imagine the bus is your confinement. Imagine the rain is your obstacle. Listen as I tell you to stop thinking about the weather and to let that be the concern of others.

Now, from wherever you might be, step off the bus, find your starting line, and just race.

CHAPTER 4:

DILIGENCE

CONSTANT AND EARNEST EFFORT

———————●▶———————

I watched her first high school race in the fall of 2003. She stood on that starting line without any expectations. I also watched her last high school race; she crossed the finish line of a journey that transformed her life.

Between her first race and her last, she found peace on the trails where she ran. She tested herself and overcame fears. She learned what it feels like to go beyond her wildest dreams, and she learned to deal with the disappointment of falling short. Each race offered its own challenge, each run a new opportunity. From the firing of that first starter's pistol to the very last home stretch, she grew with each passing stride.

Why is it that I watched her so closely? Well, I guess it's because I love her so much. It's because the sun rises and falls around her. It's because I was the first person to hold her the day I became her Dad.

My daughter excelled in school. She took courses that challenged her, and she responded to those challenges. She held leadership positions and earned the respect of her teachers and her peers. After high school, she went on to a prestigious college.

There will be times when what she learned in the classroom will not have prepared her for what lies ahead. There will be days when the workload is heavy, and the deadlines are looming. There will be days when nothing is going right, and success seems impossible. But she's ready for that, too.

She knows what it feels like to be in over her head and find the courage to get through. She knows that even when the hill seems to go on forever, there's a downhill on the other side. She knows that no matter how hard things may seem, the finish line lies ahead.

She has discipline and she knows that things of value aren't earned without sacrifice. Her greatest strength lies deep inside her, and she knows where to find it. So, when knowledge and reason and critical thinking just aren't enough, she has more than what she needs to muscle through.

Some time ago, we took a run together. We were on an isolated trail, and the only things near us were things you can find in any forest or near any lake. The miles passed easily as we talked about whatever it was that came to mind. It was peaceful, and any trouble we were facing just got further and further behind us.

And so, if all else fails, she knows she has that too – the freedom to put it all behind her, clear her lungs and her mind, and come back with a fresh perspective. What could be more valuable than that?

I miss her. There is an emptiness not easily filled. I'll get over it in time, I know. And as I watch her run off toward what lies ahead, I know she's ready for whatever she finds. After all, my daughter is a runner.

I started running in 1976, at a time when the American running boom was surging. Back then, Americans were competing with the best in the world, and I remember watching Frank Shorter enter the Olympic stadium in Montreal to win the silver medal. That was mildly disappointing after he had won the gold four years earlier in Munich.

Shorter was followed by a string of great American distance runners. Bill Rodgers, who had won the Boston Marathon for the first time in 1975, joined Shorter on the 1976 Olympic team and went on to win Boston three more times in 1978, '79 and '80. Then there was Alberto Salazar, who would dominate the marathon distance, winning New York for three consecutive years from 1980 through 1982.

Among all the great distance runners of that time, I remember admiring Craig Virgin the most. In 1980, Virgin was the first, and still only, American to win the world cross-country title. He would do it again in 1981, the same year he finished second at Boston.

There was something else about Virgin, and I remembered it recently when I found an old video of him on the Internet. In the film, he was pulling away to win the 1981 Peachtree 10K in an American record time. As I watched it, it reminded me of – me.

Virgin and I looked alike. My own father once saw a picture of him in Running Times Magazine and thought he was looking at a picture of his own son. There was something inspiring about that. I guess I figured if I looked like him, maybe I could run like him too.

I spent many years trying. In the years that Virgin was winning races like Peachtree, I was beginning a string of local road racing wins. With each victory, my goals would elevate, and before long I was thinking I had a shot to run an Olympic Trials qualifying time.

It was a stretch, to say the least, but I was getting better every year and that goal kept me pressing forward.

It was a stress fracture that ended the string of successes. After that, life's changes pulled me away from running, and my focus was gone.

It was too difficult to dwell on giving up. From late childhood through my twenties, I wanted to be the next Craig Virgin, or at least the next closest thing.

What took me years to realize is this: that's not really what I wanted. I mean, I've never even met him. And while I'm sure he's a great guy, all I really know is that he ran fast. Still, all those years of wanting to be like him helped me do something pretty valuable. It helped me become me.

We all need role models. They inspire us. They give us direction, but it's important to follow them only until we discover our own way. Once we do that, we can lead instead of follow, and if we're lucky, become a role model ourselves.

Cold rain is the worst weather to run in, and it was thirty-eight degrees and raining right outside my window. I watched it, wishing I didn't have a run planned.

In Maryland, the spring and fall offer the best running weather. The moderate temperatures feel perfect when contrasted with the extremes of the preceding seasons. On those days, I can't wait to get outside.

Of course, the transitional seasons have bad days as well. Temperatures go up and down, and dreariness moves in and out. Sometimes, it almost feels like summertime, when the weight of the damp heat makes me feel sluggish no matter how fit I am.

The truth is, if you tracked the weather throughout the year, there are really only a handful of perfect running days. So, I'm used to running in less-than-ideal conditions. I learned a long time ago that if I let the weather become an excuse, then I could find at least a hundred other excuses not to run. Excuses don't serve you well if there's something you hope to gain through persistence.

So, I stepped out into the rain. It wasn't any more pleasant than I imagined it would be. A hard breeze struck me with the first stride, and the rain stung my face. There wouldn't be any easing in to this run. I needed to move fast to warm up.

And I did warm up after ten minutes or so. By then, the rain was more of a nuisance than a hindrance, and I was moving along in relative comfort.

That's the way it is when you're facing something difficult. The hardest part is almost always the very first step. Once you're moving in the right direction, momentum becomes a friend.

People passing in their cars didn't understand. They looked at me with curiosity, wondering why anyone would willingly be outside. They had no idea I was feeling comfortable, the hardest part of the run well behind me.

I eased through the final mile and turned onto my street, stopping at my driveway. I felt a sense of gratification and even stood for a few moments feeling the rain fall before going back inside.

If you are like me, you probably reflect on the past every once in a while. Time passes quickly, and it is easy to think that we've lost the promise of days past. Sometimes, that kind of reflection can lead to regret. Don't let it.

Instead, focus on the years ahead and the unwritten chapters of your life. What is it that you want to do? And perhaps more importantly, who is it that you want to become? Now is a time to imagine and to dream, not to lament.

When you do dream, paint a picture of yourself in the fulfillment of your vision. Let that picture preside over the days ahead because, rest assured, you'll need the motivation when the cold rain comes. And it will come, forming an obstacle between you and your dream. Move ahead in spite of it. Its sting is temporary, but the gratification that comes from running through it endures.

CHAPTER 5:

DISCIPLINE

THE TRAIT OF BEING UNDER CONTROL

It was four o'clock on a Friday afternoon, and I decided to leave the pressure of the workweek a little earlier than normal. I grabbed my running bag and walked towards the locker room in my office building.

I was celebrating a promotion, a milestone I didn't think I'd reach in my career, and a short run at the end of the workweek seemed like an appropriate self-indulgence.

As I began my run, I had no company on the pathway except for the flock of geese that scattered as I approached. They flew to the middle of a large pond, and as they hit the icy water, I was glad I wasn't one of them.

I didn't have any particular route planned. Instead, I wandered from place to place. I ran past the track where I've done some of my hardest workouts and by the trail where I've found peace away from many hectic mornings.

I was running easily, trying to reflect on what I had just accomplished, and in the middle of the run something unexpected occurred to me. My run wasn't as much a celebration as it was a tribute to the thing that has contributed more to my personal success than anything else I can name.

Based on my education and background, I've climbed much higher up the corporate ladder than I ever should have, and I have the discipline of running to thank for that.

I never once believed that someone or something else was responsible for my success. Running taught me long ago that there is danger in that kind of thinking. The moment you leave your future in the hands of things outside of your control, is the moment you place it in the hands of circumstance. And circumstance doesn't much care about your success.

Running has also taught me that adversity is better faced head-on than avoided. The hill in front of you won't go away, but it's easy enough to put it behind you if you just press harder for a while. Call it discipline or call it determination; without it, you won't get very far.

That lesson isn't taught enough, and too many people never realize that sacrifice is a requirement of life. You either sacrifice today to reach tomorrow's goals, or you give up your dreams in favor of the fleeting comfort that's distracting you. The pleasant reality, for those who choose the former, is that comfort is abundant when long-term goals are achieved.

When my run was finished, I went back inside and took a quick shower. I walked back to my office to grab my briefcase before heading home. I said goodbye, wondering if anyone even noticed that I had been gone during my run.

The following Monday, when I arrived back at work, I looked outside my office window and saw the geese gathered around the pond. I watched them for a few moments before getting my day started.

As I went about my morning, I faced pressing challenges, gave guidance to the people around me and tried to create a vision for what lies ahead.

Then, when lunchtime rolled around, I grabbed my running bag and spent some time strengthening the disciplines through which I've earned the privilege to do all those things.

Each fall, as the long evenings of summer suddenly fade, I'm reminded that time is passing more quickly than I realized.

Of course, time is a constant; it ticks away at the same pace it always has. A minute is still sixty seconds, just like it was when the first flower bloomed in the spring. Distance is another constant; a mile is 1,760 yards away, no matter which direction you travel. It always has been and always will be.

Running brings together these two great constants, time and distance. It's pure that way. Running, simply put, is about the measurement of time and distance.

There's something reassuring to me about that. I'm not sure what it is, but in a world that seems too complex, I'm glad that I can define my passion in simple terms.

And yet, as simple as running may be, there is something complex about the runner. Each individual comes to running with different dreams, unique motivations, and personal challenges. And each one seeks to explore his own potential by measuring himself against distance and time.

Discovering potential as a runner isn't easy; potential has a way of hiding itself. Sometimes, it can take years of hard work just to begin to recognize it. Then, even after decades of running, the runner never really knows if his potential has been reached, which may be why so many of us have a deep-rooted need to keep running.

The purity of running and the complexity of the runner are things that transcend generations. Recently, I had a chance to meet a small group of young, dedicated runners. The discussion turned, as it does many times, to the subject of racing times.

In an instant, each one of us could appreciate the accomplishments of the others because a mile and a minute are the same today as they were years ago. And because every runner understands what it takes to develop potential.

We all need to measure ourselves in one way or another. Some resist, afraid of what the outcome might be, but I think they're selling themselves short. Almost without exception, each individual's potential goes beyond his own expectations, and potential can only be reached by those willing to measure progress towards it.

Maybe runners have it easy. Time and distance are easy to measure. Personal growth, on the other hand, is harder to assess, but I've learned through running that growth in one way naturally leads to growth in another. After all, as you watch a tree reach ever closer toward the sky, don't you understand that the roots are growing stronger and deeper as well?

The transition between the seasons always reminds me that time keeps moving forward. Whenever that happens, I remember how important it is for me to set a goal, and to then measure my progress towards it.

Two runners live inside me. The first one runs without effort, smooth and fast. He is focused, his energy channeled with precision, wanting only to improve.

He is a fierce competitor, daring and tenacious. He lives for brief, glorious moments, like the instant when a competitor's footfalls first begin to fade behind him. His expectations are unquenchable. Seldom is he satisfied, even when he wins.

I remember how he led me to running back in high school, that first race when he helped me keep pace with the older runners. And later, he pushed me far beyond my expectations, each race another chance to prove something more.

It would be easy now for him to dismiss me; I can't offer what he needs. He stays nonetheless, encouraging me to try.

The second runner can go for miles without thinking once about speed. He thrives on the motion, the simple rhythm that makes him feel at home. He seeks peace, not recognition.

Through his eyes, I've watched beautiful scenes, pastures, mountains and wildlife that the first runner would scurry past. There are times when he'll stop, just to spend a few extra moments fixed within the gaze of a deer.

He was born from the first. He never would have existed without him, and yet he's matured far beyond his predecessor. He is wise, understanding the connections between running and life. And so, each run is a simple pleasure, just as each day is another gift to a life.

Independently, I am forever bonded with both runners, but when they come together there is conflict. I feel torn, wrestling with our relationship like a parent wrestles with sibling rivalry. I try to compromise, but with little influence. I suffer the yearnings of the first runner and minimize the wisdom of the second.

I have relied on the second runner for a long time now as injury and age have cursed me with limitation. And, in an irony I can't exactly explain, it is he who has gifted me with the patience I needed to persist long enough to give the first runner new life.

During the years when the injuries threatened to take running from me, it was he who gave me reasons to keep going. It was he who showed me that I can endure more miles when I don't press on every run. Because of him, I have a new base of fitness. I feel ready to consider racing again.

I need them both. I must find a way to bring them together, to resolve their differences and make them one. It won't be easy, but running has taught me that nothing worthwhile ever is.

Perhaps I can be disciplined enough to take the best from each of them. I can find the peace that my busy life so desperately demands and still have brilliant moments, when my stride opens up and I run free. And if I am successful, it can be better than it's ever been before.

McDaniel College cross-country coach Doug Renner understands the allure of college running. That's why he welcomes adult runners to his team's first home meet each year. Aside from the sprinkling of older runners, the meet in September 2010 looked much like any other college meet.

There were clusters of color as the teams warmed up, each group going through a scripted routine. Moments before the start, they all gathered behind the line, taking turns striding out until the starter called them back.

The start looked more like a sprint than a cross-county race, as runners vied for position. Then the pack moved in unison, swiftly heading toward the first turn.

At this point in a race, all dreams were alive, which caused many runners to abandon reason. The pace stayed fast, and by the time the leaders reached the one-mile mark, everyone near the front was adjusting to the fatigue from the early pace.

Almost unnoticed, running in about thirtieth place, was Steve Kartalia. At forty-five years of age, Steve had learned a few things about successful racing. He knew the pace he could maintain on this particular course, so that's the pace he settled into from the start.

As the race progressed, runners struggled to various degrees. Some slowed noticeably, others less so, but almost everyone slowed, except Steve. One by one, he passed the runners in front of him, and inched toward the lead pack as it approached the two-mile mark.

There was a long climb at this point in the race, and Steve settled just behind the leaders as they moved up the hill. At the top everyone labored, but Steve knew that opportunity was upon him, so he surged.

He accelerated to a pace he thought he could sustain to the finish, pulling away from the others. Young legs are gifted with speed, and he knew he couldn't win a sprint to the finish, so he worked to open up a lead.

As he entered the final stretch, he heard the crowd begin to cheer the runners behind him, and he knew they were racing one another. Soon he heard the footsteps approaching, but their sprint wasn't enough. Steve won the race, just one second ahead of the second runner.

In a conversation afterwards, Steve admitted that more than a few other runners in the field were capable of beating him that day. That may be true, but capability doesn't always preside over outcomes.

The components of accomplishment seldom peak together. The potential of youth lacks the wisdom of experience and vice-versa. A lot of people struggle with that, spending time either missing what they've lost or wanting what they've yet to gain.

"Thou shalt not covet" is a wise commandment. You won't gain any advantage wanting what the competition has.

Instead, gather the blessings you have on hand. Nurture them. Invest effort in making them stronger. Then, bring them with you on race day.

CHAPTER 6:

DETERMINATION

FIRMNESS OF PURPOSE

Bob Ward didn't want his parents to see his final college race in 2002. He didn't think they would want to watch it, so he asked them not to come. Looking back now, he regrets that more than anything.

A few months earlier, during his senior indoor track season for Widener University, he had done some of the best racing of his life. Having already qualified to compete in the 800-meter race at the outdoor conference meet, he was hoping to help his team win its fourth straight conference championship.

He spent the week between seasons at home on spring break. While there, he used the time to get some distance runs in as he prepared to start his final track season, but his last run before heading back to Widener would change the course of things.

A truck failed to stop at a red light. Bob doesn't know much more than that, except that he was in its path. The police report said it was going fifty miles an hour when it hit him. I spoke to one of Bob's friends, a paramedic, who was on the scene and didn't recognize him at first. He wondered if Bob would survive as he watched the Medevac helicopter carry him away.

His injuries were extensive, but he was in the best shape of his life, and that helped him recover at a rate that surprised everyone. Still, a broken femur made the doctors caution Bob against considering anything more than walking as a goal.

He was sent home with a wheelchair and a set of crutches, and two days later, with the help of his father, he went outside to hobble along the sidewalk on the crutches. That's the moment he decided he wanted to join his team and run at the conference meet.

Even after he returned to college, the most optimistic doctor told him it would take six months before he could run again. But each day, Bob was dedicated to his therapy, knowing he couldn't run until his doctors gave their approval. Finally, just before the championship meet, they did.

You can imagine the scene as Bob walked towards the starting line. Everyone in the stadium seemed to know his story, and they lined the track waiting to encourage him.

The 800-meter distance is just a two-lap race. The most amazing fact is that Bob wasn't lapped. He doesn't even remember the pain, because the adrenalin and the crowd shielded him as he ran the slowest but most heroic race of his life.

We tend to celebrate the victorious, people who give us stunning performances. It's fitting that we do this. After all, champions help us envision our own potential. On the other hand, gold medals tarnish, as do the reputations of far too many of the people who win them. Maybe that's why I've come to value the inspiring over the accomplished, humility more than triumph.

I can't tell you how many people Bob inspired that day, other than to say it was many. And while few even remember the names of the champions, everyone who was there remembers Bob's race. He only wishes his parents were among them. In some larger sense, though, I'm certain they were.

I didn't recognize the name of the sender, but the postmark showed that it was from Pittsburgh. Whatever was inside, it had traveled more than 200 miles to reach me.

The card contained a hand-written note from the mother of a runner I coach. She told me that she enjoyed my running column and expressed appreciation for my support of her daughter's running. It was a nice surprise.

I first met her daughter, Danielle Schwessinger, when she joined the Flying Feet Summer Running program. She had been running for a while, but not as regularly as she wanted. Through the summer, her mileage increased every week and she surpassed her own goal. It was a pleasure watching her fitness improve and her love of running grow.

When Danielle joined the fall program, I was impressed to learn that she wanted to run a ten-mile race. It was a lofty goal for someone with her limited running experience, but it didn't take long to realize that she was up to the challenge.

When I told Danielle about the note, I began to understand why her mother had such appreciation for my running program. Danielle's father had been diagnosed with lung cancer when she was just sixteen years old, and from her mom's perspective, running was a means to a long, healthy life.

Her father had been a strong provider – a driven man. He worked long hours to achieve success. It was only in the months of his illness that Danielle had gotten to know him well. She came to admire his strength and his sense of humor, and then he was gone.

To avoid the pain, Danielle immersed herself in the hard work of a student. It was only after college that life forced her to slow down and deal with the loss. That's when she started to run.

Running gave her peaceful time to reflect. She began feeling better physically and emotionally. And, most surprisingly, there were times when she felt her dad running beside her, as if he were there again, encouraging her along.

I have to wonder if he somehow planted the idea to run ten miles. Maybe he understood that his daughter needed a goal to pursue. Maybe he wanted her to discover her own full potential. Perhaps he wanted her to experience life in ways he never could.

It traveled 200 miles to reach me - a note that delivered a story I didn't understand at first.

We all have a story, don't we? For most of us, it speaks of challenge. Life is never easy, even for the most fortunate among us. I've come to realize that this is how it's supposed to be. It is only through struggle that we grow.

Danielle has discovered what many runners have learned before her – running strengthens a spirit. It builds courage. It prepares a person for the challenges of life.

As she crossed the finish line, the soul of a man with nicotine-black lungs breathed once again to whisper a message of love into the heart of his daughter. Now, she runs on with a sense of satisfaction, finally knowing how proud he's always been.

The pain was worse than I wanted it to be, and it came on more quickly than I expected. Just half way through the 5K race, I was suffering.

The leader was off in the distance, almost out of site, and the third-place runner was far behind me. I was going to hold my place, so the only question was this – How much pain was I willing to endure for the sake of a better finishing time?

When I think back to my competitive days, I don't remember that racing hurt so much, but I wonder if that's just the result of a fading memory. Perhaps I was simply more intimately acquainted with the pain; I haven't raced much in recent years.

The only advantage I have now is an understanding of what the pain of racing really is and how it develops. Pain, like most everything else associated with our bodies, is the work of the mind. In a sense, it is simply a warning signal. "If you don't pay attention to this," the brain tells us, "something bad might happen."

Our brain is very good at what it does. Its messages are never tardy. In fact, it sends warnings far in advance of any real danger.

I was already slowing as I ran passed the two-mile mark. By then, I was conversing with the pain, trying to make a deal. "I'll keep the pace here," I offered, "if you stay right where you are." And, that's what I did, spending the rest of the race negotiating.

No one at the finish line was aware. Pain is personal; only I knew that discomfort had stolen the best of me.

I registered quickly for the next 5K. I needed a rematch, a chance at redemption, because surrendering isn't a good option.

Once you surrender, you become your own worst enemy. You plant seeds of doubt and then wonder why the roots have grown so deep. Before long, you begin to sabotage yourself before you even get to the starting line.

Racing can be painful. Life can be more so. It is better to face it, to run through it, so that you can realize that the anticipation is worse than the experience.

The only alternative is retreat, and while many would say withdrawal is the best option, I don't believe that's true. Fear is a poor sanctuary. Courage is a better one

CHAPTER 7:

RESILIENCE

THE ABILITY TO RECOVER

———————◆ ▬———————

It was a simple compliment. Dave Herlocker was saying goodbye to me after I had directed a local race, and he said matter-of-factly, "You're a good man, Dave." I don't know why, but I've never forgotten that. I guess compliments mean the most when they come from someone you respect.

The depth of my admiration for Dave was formed in a unique way, and I can place it back to a specific morning in 1995 that began with the thumping of a Medevac helicopter passing over my house. As I sat at my breakfast table that morning, I didn't understand the significance of the moment. I simply sat and listened to it slowly fade away; but I haven't heard the sound since without thinking about Dave.

Earlier that morning, he was running with his buddies. It was a frequent routine. They would talk about their lives, throw verbal jabs and laugh as they ran. Then they would move on to start a normal day, but this particular day wouldn't be ordinary.

The accident must have happened in the moments just before I heard the helicopter. The driver had been drowsy for a while before falling asleep. His car swerved across the road, then onto the shoulder, where Dave and his friend Terry ran. Dave, who was running just ahead, was hit first and then violently pushed into Terry.

Those who were on the scene said that the paramedics worked frantically on Dave, while Terry seemed to be in better shape, even standing up on his own. Later, at the hospital, Dave continued to fight for his life when the most surprising news of all came – Terry didn't make it. I began preparing myself to lose two friends, but Dave surprised us all. He fought on like a runner.

The months that followed were harder than anyone should be asked to endure, but he would somehow live through it all. Still, as if the pain wasn't enough, the accident required another unfair sacrifice; Dave would never run again.

I can only imagine how much he must have missed it. And yet, you couldn't tell from being around him. He returned to be the heart and soul of the Westminster Road Runners Club. He directed or helped at nearly every local race and shared the excitement of any running accomplishment that was achieved by a local runner. Dave's effort and passion moved through my running community like blood runs through our veins.

Many mornings, I saw Dave taking a long, brisk walk with his dogs. It didn't matter what the conditions were; Dave's runner's heart brought him out with an inspiring dedication. Even more remarkably, he would compete in many events, usually starting ahead of the runners to avoid making the finish line crew wait for him to finish. I watched many times as Dave pressed his limits, needing still to get the very best from himself.

Whenever I've seen Dave limping towards me, I've realized that I was watching one of the strongest and bravest men I've known. And each time I've wondered if I possess the same incredible endurance that allowed him to survive and succeed through such tragedy. The answer has always been the same – I don't think so.

I can't hear the thumping of a Medevac helicopter without remembering that morning long ago. And now, there's another morning I'll remember with even more sadness.

I was reading email like I normally do before getting my day started, and I saw an email on the list with a title that simply read "Dave Herlocker." I was scared to open it, and it turned out my instinct held true. Dave had passed away quietly in his home.

It seems ironic that a man who fought so hard to live through tragedy would pass on in peaceful sleep. Life really is curious while you're living it.

The curiosities of this life are behind Dave now, just like the pain he's endured. And if I close my eyes, I can see him smiling as he stands on his old runner's legs. Can you imagine the exhilaration he must feel?

Now the pain is in those he left behind. For me, it is eased as I imagine what Dave is doing at this very moment. He's with Terry, bringing him up-to-date on everything new. They're laughing and teasing as they take the longest, fastest and best run they've ever shared.

Thanks for that compliment, Dave. I'll never forget it. And if it's not too much trouble, make a note on some future calendar so that we can take a long run together and so that I can return the favor.

Patti hated the hill, but she couldn't take a run without having to climb it. Her house stood at the crest.

This day, as she saw it looming in front of her, she wasn't sure she could make it up. She felt weak, her strength left back at the house where she had been fighting again with her teenage son. They had lived alone now for almost a year, and it hadn't been easy.

The hill was nearly a mile long, mostly gradual. There were a couple places where it leveled off, and there was a steep rise near the top. She approached it thinking how hard things had been and wanting to give up, even stopping at the foot of it.

She stood listening to her breath break the silence of the morning. Clouds drifted from her mouth with each exhale, and she watched them float off and disappear. She wished she could disappear like that.

The first step was just as sluggish as the last one, and she felt the hill pushing against her. She had no choice but to push back, and a small burst of energy came from somewhere just before she made it to the first plateau.

She relaxed for a few moments before the hill began to climb again, and then she felt a surge of emotion rise inside herself. She heard her own voice say, "Damn this hill."

Her speed was nearly twice what it had been, determination pushing her forward. Her arms pumped with each stride, punching the air. She didn't back off at the next plateau, and she felt herself accelerate as she came to the last rise.

Suddenly, she felt good, soothed by the rhythm of the motion. She looked to the side and watched the trees speed by as she passed, then looked ahead to the final, steep climb.

She was almost sprinting when she made the crest and considered continuing on past the house, before she thought about her son again. She should get back inside.

She stood in her driveway looking back at the hill as her breathing settled down. She thought about the irony. How could she be void of energy at the bottom of the hill and filled with it at the top? She didn't know. All she could think was, "Maybe I don't hate that hill as much as I thought I did."

As she turned toward the house, she saw the face of her son in the window. She stopped, smiling as it dawned on her – he has his own hills to climb.

As she stepped into the house and towards her son, she remembered why she started running almost a year ago. She needed the brief escape and the peaceful air. Now, she knew she was getting that and more.

She hugged her son, and they spoke together like they hadn't spoken in a long time. They talked about hills.

I was the smallest boy in any group when I was growing up. I sat in the front row of every elementary class picture I have. My best friend towered over me.

I was well aware that I was little, but never gave it much thought when it came to the things I wanted to do. In my dreams I could do anything.

Reality didn't always match my expectations. Once, a fly ball landed on my face. Bigger boys threw fastballs past my late swing. I failed a lot.

There came a time when extra effort and some amount of natural athleticism compensated for my size. I ran down fly balls and learned how to hit. I had a good jump shot as long as no one was there to block it.   In middle school, I made a diving catch in the end-zone to win a football game for my gym class team.

Still, I think I was the only person who considered me an athlete.

By the time I started running, I understood what it felt like to be overlooked. I knew that losing hurt. I realized that every other person in the game was hoping to outperform me. In other words, I knew what it was like to live in this world of ours.

It was that understanding that sparked my determination. I missed favorite TV shows without being able to DVR them. I shivered through the first lonely miles of winter runs. I pushed myself so hard in workouts that I went to sleep with throbbing legs.

One year, I spent six months doing my workouts in cold water, which I hated, because I couldn't run through an injury.

I tasted enough success to see progress but got dusted even more. It was the times I was tromped, not the times I won, that fueled me.

If I had been born a few decades later, I may have been different. Someone would have given me a trophy for showing up, and I might have been satisfied. I might have gotten the message that someone or something else was responsible for my performance, or lack thereof.

My last competitive racing season was the spring of 1989, and my final race of that season came in May. Four miles into that 10K race, I was with the leaders, using every ounce of my strength to hang on. In the final miles the ultimate winner surged, and I struggled home in fourth place, unsatisfied.

I spent five months of focused training preparing to win that race and, at the time, it was more than a little frustrating. Looking back now, though, I understand that it was my willingness to risk losing that gave me the courage to try to win.

Without failure, there is no success.

My first running buddy was a miniature schnauzer named Pepper. Pepper was my childhood dog, my companion growing up. I only remember a few things about Pepper, the most important of which is how I felt about him. We shared a special bond like many young boys and their dogs.

He was chosen as my running buddy by default. There was no one else who wanted to play running with me, so he joined in, though reluctantly at times.

The race course consisted of circles around our house. Given that Pepper was on a leash and didn't know how many laps were in the race, I had a distinct advantage. He would normally run a few yards ahead, and then I would heroically sprint past him just before the finish line. We would celebrate together, the winner and the runner-up.

I'm not sure how old Pepper was when he got sick. All I remember is sitting at the table crying with my mother and sister as my father carried him out of the house. He died before I got to high school and became a real runner.

Growing up is hard; I doubt anyone would dispute that. Relationships are risky from the beginning. Friends come and go with the passing of school years and the making of young decisions. It's no wonder we all struggle through that time as we search for affirmation through other kids who are mostly incapable of giving it. In times when I needed it most, Pepper was waiting.

The first gift running provided was the blessing of self-confidence. I faced challenges. I struggled, but I overcame them and found success. The days of needing someone else to assure me were past.

Later, when I was learning to live with the pressure of life's routines and deadlines, running gave me stability in a changing world. Every day there was a break in the madness when I went outside to play.

Running gave me freedom. It let me dream. It formed a bridge between my childhood and adulthood that helped me keep my identity as my peers were losing theirs.

When my kids were young, it seemed natural to get a dog for them. We chose a bischon because it seemed like the breed was a perfect match for our family. We named him Forrest after the then-famous runner Forrest Gump.

Not surprisingly, Forrest formed a strong bond with my son. Forrest is to him as Pepper was to me.

Forrest was fourteen when he began showing signs that the end was coming. Soon afterwards, life repeated itself like it does sometimes, and I became the father carrying the dog away as my wife and kids watched with tears in their eyes.

Even if we don't realize it, the pieces of life are connected together. Our childhood, our relationships, and our experiences live on in us, even after they've passed. I've come to understand that, for some, those memories form anchors, holding them in place as life passes by.

Somehow, I've managed to keep all of life's challenges in perspective and keep moving forward, and I have running to thank for that

CHAPTER 8:

PATIENCE

ABILITY TO ENDURE DELAY

———————◄ ►———————

This story isn't over, just so you know. The final chapters will only be written in time.

I'll begin the telling with a photograph, taken just moments before the start of the 2009 Baltimore Half-Marathon. Julie Peatt is with the rest of the runners I coach, easy to spot wearing a purple birthday hat. It was her 46th birthday, and the day was made even more special because she had missed this race the year before. After having trained since early summer 2008, a hip injury made it impossible for her to run.

The day before the 2009 race, Julie browsed through the exhibits at the runner's expo looking for a meaningful souvenir. She found two: a magnet with a quote from John Bingham that reads "The miracle isn't that I finished - The miracle is that I had the courage to start," and a bracelet with the inscription "Trust the journey." She's worn the bracelet nearly every day since.

After the picture was taken, Julie went to the starting line with her running partners. If you've never been to an event like this one, you'll have a hard time imagining the experience. Thousands of runners were waiting for a moment that had taken months, sometimes years, to prepare for. When the race finally began, the burden of apprehension was collectively lifted from the crowd.

Julie and her partners began easy, remembering not to get caught up in the excitement. There was a point early on when a motivating song played over the crowd, and Julie pulled away briefly before regaining control and slowing down to re-join her friends.

By the time she got to mile seven, a familiar pain in her hip was becoming increasingly uncomfortable. As she passed mile eight, it was impossible to ignore. Just before mile nine, severe pain stopped her in her tracks. Her hip labrum, the cartilage lining the hip socket, had torn.

The events that followed were blurry. There was a period of walking and jogging when Julie tried to convince herself she could still finish. Friends would pass, and she urged them on, telling them that she would see them at the end. There was an old college friend at a water stop and a couple police officers who offered to help. Finally, a running friend made her face the reality – she needed to stop.

There is another photograph from that day, taken as she waited in the ambulance, waving to the camera and still wearing the purple birthday hat. That picture, as much as anything else, tells you something about Julie.

It doesn't really matter that she didn't finish. She did have the courage to start, which is far more important. Too many times, we're unwilling to leave the safety of our comfort zone, and that confinement places a greater limitation on our lives than any other thing.

And once you do find the courage, understand that you may never reach your destination - but that's okay. A destination marks a moment in time, a brief conclusion, but the journey is life itself.

Cautiously, Julie returned to running, living the final chapters of an unfinished story and trusting the journey as she goes.

I had to stop. The urge was so strong that I didn't want to fight it anymore. So, I did - stop running, that is.

I didn't realize it was going to be a bad run when I started. It began much like most of my other midweek, lunchtime runs. All I was looking for was a quiet escape from the morning rush, and I ran slowly, moving towards my favorite trail.

Before I had even finished the first mile, I could tell I wasn't going to be picking up the pace. My legs were heavy. My breathing was labored. I tried to distract myself by looking at the landscape, but it didn't help very much.

I made it to the point where I turn around, and I started heading back. I wondered why I was struggling, when just the day before my run had been a good one. I had felt relaxed and fast, which reminded me of my running before the accumulating years slowed me down.

I knew well enough, after decades of running, that sometimes I simply won't know exactly what it is that's slowing me. It could be emotions or restless sleep. It could be the remnants of greasy food from days before, still lingering in the muscles I was asking to propel me forward. Whatever the reason, there was nothing that I could do to change it.

And so, I was left with a single choice: to accept it. Less than a mile from finishing, I stopped.

I walked slowly along the pathway, listening to my breathing settle down. As it faded, I heard the playful noise of nature rising – a simple joy that always exists for those who look closely enough.

When I was younger, I never would have allowed myself the pleasure of backing off. I would have thought I was weak for doing so. Now, I think I'm a little wiser. Energy is a limited resource and investing it foolishly has never gotten me very far.

It's taken me longer than it should have, but I've finally learned that bad days are simply a part of the deal. You can't win unless you're willing to lose. And, though most people never sort through the irony, you can't take control of your life until you're willing to accept that some things are simply outside of your control.

No one ever achieved anything by applying their effort or worry towards something they can't influence. After all, you can't move an ocean, no matter how large your bucket might be. Success, then, is only achieved by continually channeling your energy towards the things you can influence, like making sure you start moving forward again after a brief reprieve.

I took a deep breath and started running again. My legs moved a bit more freely than before, and I was able to enjoy the final moments of a run I was glad to finish.

The fatigue lingered for a little while, but before long my tired run was forgotten. I moved on to more productive things and began looking forward to my next run.

He was just finishing his workout as I ran onto the track, and it just so happened that we both stopped to stretch at the same time and place. I asked him how he was doing, and I could feel the frustration in his response.

He was young, maybe 20, and I could tell he was a good runner. His talent was equaled by his passion, so my heart went out to him as he told me about the challenges he was facing.

He could hardly get through the workout he had just finished, and his times were slower than he was shooting for. It had been like that for a while, and he couldn't seem to break away from the sluggishness. He wanted it to be like it had been when he was running well and improving consistently.

When he was ready to walk away, I found myself wanting to offer something that would help, but all I could manage was, "Hang in there. Things will get better."

As I started my own workout, I began thinking about the missed opportunity. I had a chance to have an impact on this young runner, and I wondered if I had been helpful at all.

I spent the rest of my workout thinking about how I used to feel when my stride wasn't restricted by old joints. There were times when it seemed like I could have run as fast and as far as I wanted. I remember dreaming about faster times and then accomplishing the workouts that would lead toward my goals. Races were playgrounds.

I also remember when it hadn't been so easy. There were long stretches, sometimes a year or more, when I couldn't find rhythm in my running.

When my workout was over, I stopped in the same spot to stretch again, and I noticed he had left his sweatshirt behind. Just as I was about to leave, I saw him walking toward me.

There was an awkward moment as he wondered why I was waiting for him, but it dissolved in good conversation as I shared my story. I think it helped him to know that what he was going through wasn't unusual.

Then I told him something that he wasn't expecting, something he might not understand until a few more years pass by. The human spirit has a deep-rooted need to be tested, and potential can never be fully realized until the spirit is strong. So, I told him, even as hard as things seemed, he was developing in ways he might not yet fully appreciate, and the worst thing he could ever do is give up.

Some people think that life would be better if things always went exactly the way we wanted them to, but I'm not convinced that's true. Fulfillment would be hard to find in a world where success was handed out like free samples at the grocery store.

So, as you crave what you want in life, try to understand that the journey towards success is just as important as whatever prize you're chasing. After all, in the end, it's not really what you get that matters; it's what you become

CHAPTER 9:

ACCOUNTABILITY
WILLINGNESS TO ACCEPT RESPONSIBILITY

———————◄ ►———————

The September morning was a stark contrast to the summer-like days leading up to it. The air was crisp, perfect for the 10K race I was about to run.

My training had been going well. I had put in three straight weeks of sixty or more miles, something I rarely did. My track work had been strong as well, perhaps better than it had ever been before.

We started on the streets of the small town hosting the race, and the first mile led us onto country roads close by. Early on, I was letting the race unfold without much thought with the leaders running about 30 yards ahead. That's when the runner beside me said matter-of-factly – "Let's catch those guys."

Together, we surged up to the leaders, and within minutes I was controlling the pace up front. From that point on, I remember feeling like I was floating along the course. By the two-mile mark, there were just two runners struggling to hold on, and I smiled as the marshal called out the split. I knew already that the race was mine.

It's special knowing something great is happening and having time to relish the experience. I turned around at the 5K mark and began the journey back. I could feel the eyes of my competitors, and as I ran on through the fourth mile, I heard cheers from the crowd of runners still moving out towards the turnaround.

As I passed back into city limits, a police motorcycle began to escort me toward the center of town. I followed it, feeling myself picking up the pace. There was a final rise, then a descent to the finish where I couldn't help but raise my arms as I crossed the line with a personal best.

Some might say that remembering a day like that is basking in old glory, but there are more important reasons to reminisce.

Before that race, I placed limits on what I could accomplish, and I had dreams that I doubted would ever come true. Afterwards, I found a reason to believe in myself, and dreams that seemed unreachable were suddenly in the realm of possibility. Why would I want to forget a day like that?

I already knew that hard work and diligence were parts of the success equation, but I learned that day that accountability was a missing piece; I couldn't wait for someone else to tell me when it was time to run with the leaders.

Every time I look back on my best races, I find a lesson worth remembering. It's like a seed was planted each time, and it's only in looking back that I can discover what blossomed. More often than not, it's a crop worth harvesting.

Of course, there are lessons in the setbacks as well, sometimes even more valuable. I've learned through hardship that progress is a fickle thing, not showing itself when you're expecting it. When that happens, it's easy to become discouraged or even lose hope.

Don't.

Always believe that someday the stars will line up exactly the way you want them to. And even if they never do, the thrill that comes from touching those stars is only equaled by the personal satisfaction that comes from reaching for them.

I woke to a day when we had a record-breaking snowstorm. With no run planned, my only workout that day came in the form of heavy snow and a shovel.

When I was done, I stood on the back patio for a few moments admiring the scene. The snow was beautiful. There was peace in the muffled silence until I realized something was missing. There were no boot prints or sledding paths in the snow. My children had moved on.

It's funny how our day-to-day routines shelter us from a life that's constantly changing, until something stops us for a moment, so we can take an inventory. It's not like I didn't realize that my kids were getting older, but something in that moment made the fact more real.

I knew when they were born that my role as a father would be the most important of my life. And yet, there were no instructions to follow, so I've pretty much learned along the way. Making it even more difficult, there are no real ways to measure success.

Both of my children have grown to become good people; some would use that as a barometer, but they, not I, deserve the credit for that. Over the years, I've found that what I say to them has only a marginal effect. It has been their experiences, and their reactions to those experiences, that have largely shaped them.

What I've finally come to realize is that my highest purpose as a father can be described in rather simple terms - to set an example for my children to follow. Here is where running enters the story and where I have the opportunity to share something of value with you.

If you want your children to be strong, demonstrate strength. If you want them to be successful, illustrate the qualities that success requires. If you want them to be happy, show them that there is more to life than deadlines and responsibilities.

Running has allowed me to do all those things. As I've trained, overcome challenges and crossed finish lines, my children have watched me. As I've found joy and passion on my runs, they have noticed. In the process, they've learned more than they have from all the speeches, rules and punishments combined. It's not that those other things don't have an important place, but you can't guide your children with them if your own personal principles are misguided.

We all have a vision of what we'd like to become – a great athlete, a good parent, or simply a good person. Whatever your vision might be, the principles of running – things like discipline, resilience and consistency – will serve you well. And if you should ever need a little extra motivation to practice these, let it come from the eyes that are watching and following your lead.

I knew every split needed to run a ten-mile race in 55:50. In case I forgot, they were written down with ink in the palm of my hand.

I was twenty-two, and I didn't have a coach or any real training plan. The only things I understood about running were these: I had a knack for it, and the hard work was paying off. Every race was an experience of discovery.

The warm August day was just beginning to cool as a small but talented field gathered at the starting line. The first mile of the out-and-back course was gradually uphill, but my excitement pulled me through that mile in 5:19. Two runners were keeping me company, and we continued to breeze through the second mile, passing that mark in 10:34.

I realized that I was the one pressing the pace and backed off as the course began a three-mile climb towards the turnaround point. I was well ahead of my target and more than willing to bide my time until we started heading back home.

The other two runners seemed at my mercy; I relaxed, letting them linger on my shoulder. They hung there until we reached the turnaround in 27:53, two seconds faster than my goal pace.

It felt good to have the hardest part of the course behind me, and I accelerated on the downhill. Within a hundred meters, I was by myself. The runners still heading out watched me run by as mile six passed easily.

During the seventh and eighth miles, the road got quiet, and I relished the feeling of control. The final water station was at the eight-mile point, and I grabbed a cup and looked at my watch, passing the mark in 44:08. Even if I slowed considerably, I would reach my goal.

I could feel the fatigue growing during the ninth and tenth miles, but my momentum carried me as I made the final climb. I pushed through the downhill of the last mile and crossed the finish line in 55:05, glad it was over, but wishing the adrenalin high would last a little longer. The numbers in the palm of my hand were smeared in sweat, and I smiled as I wiped them away.

I'm almost embarrassed to say this, but I didn't understand how fortunate I was back then. I was blessed to be able to run away from competition and feel the unusual thrill of winning races. The bliss was almost blinding, and I would often run and race without any real plan or direction. Looking back now, I know I fell far short of my potential.

Most of us either fail to understand or fail to accept an important truism of life – the promise of today is temporary. Before you know it, something you are lucky to have will be gone.

Fortunately, wisdom is mostly gained by making mistakes, and now I fully embrace the blessings in my life, most of which are far more important than running fast.

How about you? Do you see the possibilities in front of you? Are you embracing what you love? Whatever your answer, one thing is certain. Most things fade away in time, like ink pen from a sweaty palm.

1976- GRIFFIN RUNNING IN PRACTICE
DURING HIS FIRST CROSS COUNTRY SEASON

1977- CROSS COUNTRY TEAM PHOTO
(GRIFFIN 2ⁿᵈ FROM LEFT, CENTER
ROW)

1979- GRIFFIN WINNING THE COUNTY
MILE AGAINST MD STATE CROSS COUNTRY
CHAMP KELLY LONG

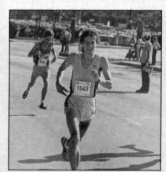

1982 - CONSTELLATION CLASSIC 10K

1984 - MARINE CORPS MARATHON

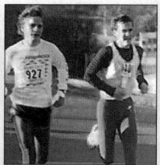

1986 - FINISHING FROSTBITE 15K
WITH JEFF SCUFFINS

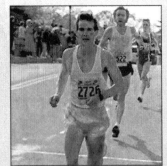

1989 - CHERRY BLOSSOM 10-MILE

2002 - B&A TRAIL MARATHON

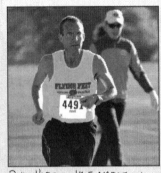

2011 - HERSHEY HALF MARATHON

2012 - FINISHING A LOCAL RACE

2017 - COACHING THE FLYING FEET
RUNNING PROGRAM

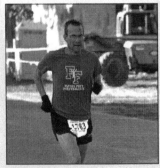

2017 - REHOBOTH HALF MARATHON

CHAPTER 9:

TRANQUILITY
SERENELY QUIET AND PEACEFUL

Just as the sun touched the horizon, a young deer moved away from the others. Exploring the edge of the woods, she found acorns that had fallen through the night. She was getting her share before the squirrels started gathering.

A few miles away, I had just started my run, stiff legs asking me to turn around. I ignored them, knowing they would stop complaining soon. Earlier, when the alarm had gone off, I wanted to keep sleeping. I had won that battle as well - two small victories.

It was a crisp morning. The world was colored with change and the air was new. I hadn't turned on the TV or the radio that morning. Nothing had spoiled the day, and it was perfect.

I remember moving along the trails, not paying much attention to my pace. You could say it was more of an exploration than a run. There was so much beauty that it was hard to take it all in. The smells of the earth reminded me of my high school years, when I ran around the corn fields and through the woods around the school.

There was no sound, except for my breath. It was almost like someone had hit the mute button on life. And in the slow rhythm of my breathing, the sights passed by like a parade, one striking picture after another.

Those runs are the best - effortless, with no thought of distance, just moving through the space around me. It was like I was a part of it all, even though I was miles from home in the middle of a place I had never been before.

I first saw her as I came around a turn. I stopped, and she looked up and stared. I know it wasn't long, but those few moments passed slowly as we both considered why we had crossed paths. Then she was gone, quickly moving back in the direction from which she had come, leaving fewer acorns for the squirrels to gather.

I stood there for a few more moments, wishing she had stayed a little longer. As I lingered, the sounds of the world returned with the breeze rustling the trees and the birds waking up.

My run was over before I wanted it to be, and I had to get my day started. There's always something that needs to be done. But the rest of my day was touched with a feeling that I was blessed. There was beauty in the world and I would see it again – soon.

It's funny how the running itself was never my motivation. That came from my competitive spirit and the desire to run fast. Now that my fastest days are well behind me, most of what I appreciate isn't about the races, but about the quiet runs.

I appreciate the peaceful feeling I find while everyone else is still in their beds and the freedom of being a part of something much bigger than myself. And, more than anything, I appreciate the paths that I cross, even if for the briefest of moments.

There's an old dirt road that winds by a swift stream and I run there sometimes. It's an isolated place and I seldom see anyone else when I'm there. It looks the same as it did when I first ran on its crushed gravel many years ago.

There are times when I run there just to remind myself that some things remain the same, which is somehow comforting to me. So much of the world is in a perpetual state of change.

People resist change, and I understand why. We find comfort in our routines and our preferences. The changes in the world around us are enough to deal with. We want our own lives to be consistent.

Over time complacency can grow. The sphere of our comfort zone shrinks, and we convince ourselves that we're too old to change.

Then something unexpected happens, something bad. It is in those times that we may resolve to do something differently, or to do something new.

As a coach, I've watched hundreds of people resolve to become runners. They each begin for a unique, personal reason but always with a common goal; they want something about their life to become better.

Each new runner battles apprehension and doubt. The challenge is hard, sometimes even painful.

But with persistence, a transformation begins. It's subtle at first. One day a run seems easier. Then a runner is surprised when she doesn't have to walk up the hill that's always beaten her before. Progress builds confidence, and before long the benefits of continuing far outweigh the false comfort of settling back into complacency.

The foundation of strength grows over time as the accomplishments mount. Two-mile runs become five-mile runs. A month of discipline becomes a year. Self-confidence extends well beyond the act of running because determination and fortitude are transferable.

At some point, though the exact moment is never certain, running becomes more than just something they do; it becomes something they are. And, in an irony I can't exactly explain, what started as a means of change becomes a pillar of stability.

For those who have run for many years, running gives even the most volatile days a familiar feel; the movement and the effort are like old friends.

The uncertainty of life can scare you if you let it. The instability can knock you down. It is only on our own foundation that we can stand strong.

And that's why I'll keep returning to that old dirt road. The beauty and the solitude calm me and remind me that I can be strong, all by myself.

You've heard of the book *The Loneliness of the Long Distance Runner*. I've never read it, but its title creates an image that I've never really understood. Perhaps one of the most treasured aspects of being a runner is having time alone to think, to feel, and to sort things out.

I remember a run on a winter morning a long time ago. I drove out to the middle of nowhere to find a quiet trail to run away on. There was a dusting of snow on the ground, and there the world was a quiet place. As I began to run, only my footfalls broke the silence.

It seemed like even the animals stayed away as I wandered through the woods that morning, though the tracks in the snow showed they were there before me. The crisp air frosted my breath and, by this time, my breathing mixed with my footfalls to create a rhythm.

I ran by fallen trees, along streams, and through pine trees. I ran over hills and through valleys. Off in the distance there was nothing more than what was right in front of me - miles and miles of solitude. I wasn't aware of speed - only movement. It was like I was daydreaming, watching the world around me but locked safely inside myself.

I ran until the weight of the world was gone. By that time, my car was miles away. It had started snowing, and the flakes made it feel like I was running in a snow globe. The peacefulness was overwhelming, and I had to stop for a while to take it all in.

Have you ever heard the sound of snowflakes landing in the forest? Have you ever felt as if the nearest person was a hundred miles away? Somehow, that day, those sounds and those feelings were exactly what I needed.

Running has always done that - given me what I need. When I was in high school I needed identity. Afterwards, I needed achievement. Some days, I've just needed a reason to be proud of myself. Running has always delivered.

I turned around and followed my footprints, returning the same way I had come. I was a bit reluctant as I approached the end, not wanting the run to be over. I glanced back as I got into my car; then I left that place feeling a thousand times better than when I had arrived.

Perhaps some would call that loneliness, but I'm not one of them. I've journeyed alone thousands of miles along the roads and trails near my home. While people I've known have spent their time searching for the things they thought would make them happy, I've spent my running time searching for what seemed more valuable to me. And as I've run, the treasures weren't found in the world around me but inside myself.

Loneliness? I guess I've never felt that. Alone? Well, sometimes that's exactly what I need to be.

I should have been used to the rain; the sun hadn't shown itself for a week. But as I ran beside Culp's Hill in Gettysburg, the dreariness seemed out of place.

Whenever I have a free day, I try to go to Gettysburg for a run. The beauty and peacefulness lure me there.

This day was different. There was a low cloud moving through the tree tops. As I ran under it, I imagined it was the ghosts of rebel soldiers assaulting the hill one last time. The gloom was unsettling.

I moved along the battle lines and passed the monuments that grace the roadside. The woods surrounding me were filled with the sounds of raindrops on leaves, but it was otherwise silent. The place was lonely.

For the first time, I had a sense of the sorrow that must have surrounded the area back in 1863. Only honor and discipline could persuade a man to do what they did; the burden of terror and misery would have otherwise led them to flee.

But they didn't flee. They stood together, each facing his own fear, and fought through what I imagine was the most difficult experience in our history, Americans butchering other Americans.

I ran to the top of Culp's Hill and then looped back down, moving past the equestrian statue of General Slocum who commanded the troops there. Then I turned onto an alleyway and ran into town where my car was waiting.

Sometime after the battle, no one knows exactly when, Private Augustus L. Coble returned to Culp's Hill in Gettysburg. Having fought on the hillside, I imagine he remembered it as a terrible place.

On a boulder that marks the position where Private Coble fought, he chiseled his name and regiment into the stone. It must have taken him hours to complete; the writing is still there.

Residing in North Carolina after the war, he lived with poverty and grief. Memorializing his place in the battle must have been a way to remind himself that he was a survivor, that he could overcome even the most horrible things.

Our own troubles may be small by comparison, but they are very real to us. There is hardship and uncertainty. Some people have lost hope. And if you don't feel it now, life will send you challenge soon enough. The sorrow of loss and the consequence of bad decisions reach all of us at one time or another.

The most important choice we have is this – do we prepare ourselves by building a character of strength or do we cower and wish the hardship away?

Everyone knows that running involves discomfort and that's why most non-runners wonder why we do it. What most don't understand is that the pain has a purpose; as we endure the suffering of our sport, we learn that we can also overcome the challenges of life.

And, in the process, we discover that there is tranquility even under the darkest cloud.

CHAPTER 11:

HUMILITY

A LACK OF FAKE PRIDE

———————

I had just finished one of the best runs I had had in a long time. There was almost no pain from my stubborn injuries and my legs were smooth and free. It felt good to run fast.

Whenever I have a run like that, my mind turns to competition. I start to think about my past success and dream about what might be possible if the injuries would loosen their hold on me.

My son, Paul, runs too, but he's never had the competitive nature of his old man. He is more than willing to accept whatever running offers him.

I was still thinking about my encouraging run when I got the phone call. Paul was ill and on his way to the emergency room. Before I could come to terms with what was happening, we were en route to Johns Hopkins Hospital where Paul could be better cared for.

The days that followed were filled with uncomfortable waiting as the doctors tried to figure out just what was making Paul sick. In those days, running hardly crossed my mind. It was only in the relief of learning that Paul was going to be fine that I packed a running bag one morning as I prepared to head down to the hospital.

That afternoon, Paul was asleep when I went outside to run a few miles. It was a different kind of run; I'm not used to city noise and endless concrete. I passed hundreds of people but didn't find one kindred running spirit, though I searched as I jogged in place waiting for traffic to pass.

I ran the city blocks around the hospital several times before I began to relax, and by the time the run was over I felt a peaceful calm that I desperately needed.

I wiped the sweat from my face as I walked back inside. I moved through the hallways and towards my son, thinking about how blessed I've been to have him in my life.

Things were hectic when he was young, but he had a way of reminding me to appreciate simple joy. I remember the belly laugh that lured me to play and the innocent wonder that led me to slow down and explore beside him.

It seems a bit ironic that he's taught me so much about life. After all, I thought I was supposed to be the teacher in the relationship. And while I've tried to share whatever wisdom I have to offer, his lessons to me have been just as valuable, if not more so.

When I walked back into his hospital room, Paul was still sleeping. I stared for a few minutes and whispered a quiet thank you.

I know myself too well to think I'm ready to stop dreaming about running fast, but it's a dream that can't live forever. When I'm finally ready to let it go, I'll take an easy run and try to keep it all in perspective, and it will help if Paul's there running beside me.

A few times each year, the runners I coach through my running program gather in Gettysburg for a run. I was on the battlefield planning the route for our next running excursion there.

After I was finished, I was getting ready to take a run myself when my cell phone rang. It was my daughter, Katie, who was then attending Gettysburg College.

She told me she had just received an email from the office of the college president, advising the students that there had been a fatal stabbing on campus. Though she wasn't in any danger, the email had been unsettling, and I think it made her feel better knowing I was close by.

When we were done talking, I started my run. Running on the battlefield has always been peaceful for me, and I can never exactly resolve the irony that peace could be so easy to find in a place that had witnessed such violence.

Still, like every time before, within minutes I was immersed in the calm beauty of the place. I ran along Confederate Avenue, where Robert E. Lee's army gathered before the famous attacks that were launched from Seminary Ridge.

I ran past trees that had borne witness to the battle and by stone monuments that told the stories of men. I ran through fields where spring flowers were just starting to show themselves and by distant mountains that watched as I passed. In the final mile, I was running hard, alive with the energy that always finds me during my runs there.

That afternoon, Katie called again. Rumors about the stabbing were beginning to surface and they all seemed to involve Emily, a girl Katie knew from her freshman year at the college. While we were on the phone, the rumors were confirmed.

Katie told me that she remembered Emily as someone who had shown her kindness at a time when kindness was something she desperately needed. As we talked, hundreds of others were sharing similar memories, each one about a giving, caring, passionate soul who left us too soon.

I wasn't very helpful in finding answers to the questions Katie had. Listening was all I could offer.

Later, my thoughts turned to the run that morning and the enduring irony about the peace I find on the battlefield at Gettysburg. In a way, life is built around that irony. Tragedy is all around us. The trick, perhaps, is to find our own peace in the midst of it.

Discovering a reason for Emily's death is impossible. Still, if we search, we might find meaning in her life. Life, after all, is always shorter than we expect it to be. Knowing that can help us realize the importance of the day we are living at this very moment. If Emily could somehow find her voice, I have a feeling she'd tell us something like that.

Maybe that's why I love my runs in Gettysburg. As I pass through humbling fields that remind me how real death is, I feel very much alive.

I haven't written much about 1986. It wasn't my best year.

It began well enough. On the very first weekend I finished fourth in a 15K race with a large, talented field. The next two weeks, I ran every day, sometimes twice, and averaged nearly eighty miles a week, high mileage for me.

On January 19th, I ran four miles to get to a local five-mile race, cruised along to win the race in 27:42, and then ran back home for a total of 13 miles. But if you look at the notes in my log that day, you'll see two prophetic words – knee sore.

By the end of March, the knee pain was worse, and I was taking short breaks. By summer, I wasn't running at all.

In the midst of all of this, I started a new job. It wasn't that I didn't like what I was doing before; I loved working at the local running store. But I didn't think my job provided opportunity for someone who hoped to support a family someday, and so I began a challenging new career in sales.

A few months later, my young marriage ended, and life devolved into a painful, confused mess.

Months of physical therapy did nothing to help my knee, and I eventually learned that surgery was necessary. Diagnostics weren't as sophisticated back then, and so there was some mystery around what the surgeon would find during the operation. But whether with or without his blessing, I began doing short runs in October.

On the day before the surgery, I ran to the Western Maryland College track. Then I stopped and sat down on the outside lane.

I consider this a low point of my life. I was lonely, failing at work, and about to lose running indefinitely.

And so, I got up and started running hard around the track.

Running has always given me a sense of freedom. The movement is liberating, like flight to a bird. And somewhere deep in the discomfort of fatigue, I become immune to all other pain.

I paid no attention to my watch. I didn't count laps. I simply ran fast until I couldn't run any more, and then I staggered to the outside lane and sat back down.

Looking back now, I think those laps were my way of staking a claim – no matter what, running would always be a part of me.

Despite my doctor's urging about a future of arthritis in my knee, I started training and racing again in 1987. I fell in love and got married in 1988. By the end of 1989, we started a family, and my hard work began to present me with new opportunities.

No challenge since has been as difficult as those I faced in 1986, but my days haven't all been easy. You know life as well as I do, so elaboration isn't necessary. In all my years, running has been the most effective remedy to any worry, stress, or pain.

But running has been more than that, because things which we persist in doing leave an imprint upon our deepest self.

I need only one word to describe myself – runner.

I'm proud of that definition. It conjures up images of discipline and effort. And yet, I'm in a process of evolution, and a part of me doesn't want to keep pace.

My younger self presides over my emotions too many times. He wants to run fast with the leaders. He refuses to remember the year on the calendar, pulling my aspirations back decades, and I can't seem to satisfy him.

We don't linger in the past, that's impossible, but the past often lingers in us. So how do we resolve a dispute when we ourselves are the only participant?

I know the answer, but I'm still learning to embrace it.

All our experiences and interactions are carried forward. We are at our best when we use them not as a basis for comparison, but as a source of guidance.

There are days now when I can simply enjoy this blessing I have. I immerse myself in fresh air and find comfort in the familiar rhythm. And even as I aspire to find whatever potential I have left, I want to keep running gratefully.

CHAPTER 12:

JOYFULNESS

GREAT HAPPINESS

———————————•——————————

I sorted through my clothes but couldn't find the black socks. I made a note to stop at the store on my way to the church, and then I went outside to start my run.

It was a January morning in 1988. The cold air almost stunned me, and snow covered the ground from a storm just days before, but I needed a run to calm my nerves. It was going to be a big day.

It was early, and the streets of town were vacant. As I moved past the buildings, I could see my reflection in the windows from the corner of my eye, and I couldn't resist the urge to watch myself. It felt good to be running well again.

The year before had been difficult. In a blessed life, it's the one time I'd rather forget. As if the days weren't already hard enough, I had to face them without running because I was enduring a serious injury. Since the pavement was off limits, I found myself in the pool to maintain my fitness.

It was in the midst of all of this that I first met her. I remember the moment vividly. She introduced herself as I was walking to the locker room. We talked briefly before going our separate ways, but we said hello every time we saw each other after that. Before long, I was looking for her whenever I went to the club for a workout.

As I continued running through town that day, I saw her apartment in the distance. For a moment I considered stopping, but afraid she might still be sleeping, I ran past.

My pace quickened as I headed back home, and I realized the tempo would have been impossible just months before. Progress had been slow after the injury, but I was starting to set goals again. To a competitive distance runner, goals equal survival. The hard work is impossible without understanding what's at stake. And by this time, I was working hard for both of us. I wanted her to be proud of me.

When the run was over, I walked for a while before going back inside. I've always enjoyed the quiet of morning, and the peaceful feeling was going to stay with me for a long time. I wasn't likely to forget anything about this particular run.

I showered, shaved, and got dressed. I stared at the mirror for a few moments thinking how much I hated the tuxedo, but I knew she'd think I looked handsome. I stopped by the store for the black socks, and then went on to the church.

In the years between then and now, I've smiled at the irony many times. It was in the midst of heartache that I found my greatest love.

It seems somehow appropriate that it was running that led me in the right direction at a time when I didn't know where I was headed. Maybe you've noticed - running is the thread that holds most of the pieces of my life together. She holds all the rest.

All days were long days. The sun arose in the morning sky and stayed there, or at least that's how it seemed to me.

While the working people would have hated my long days, I was a kid, and they were glorious.

There was a mud room in my basement where all the toys that a young boy needed were kept. I surveyed all of them, deciding what I wanted to play.

If I close my eyes, I can still see every inch of that room. Pegs on an unfinished wall were used to hang the jackets, elbows stiff from the dirt of a hard fall or a diving catch. I put my jacket on, grabbed a bat and ball, and then I stepped outside.

I had no deadlines looming, no bills to pay, and no relationship issues. I was free to exist in my small world in a way that made me happy.

I walked to the back of the yard where we had our baseball field.

It was a baseball field only in a makeshift way. The batter's-box and pitcher's mound were hard dirt, made by the feet of all those who played there. First base was just past the swing set, second base was in the middle of the yard and third base was a white pine tree.

The outfield fence was a row of trees that ended with a telephone pole perfectly positioned down the left-field line. There was no pole on the other side, but I batted right handed, so that didn't matter.

I stood in the batter's box, the bat on my shoulder and the ball in my left hand, waiting for my imagination to take hold. In a brief moment the opposing team appeared, complete with a pitcher winding up on the mound.

I tossed the ball, a soft lob that fell nicely into my sweet spot. The bat struck to ball hard, and it sailed to the base of the left-field fence. The outfielders gave chase. By the time they threw the ball to second base, I was safely there, the first of what would become many grass stains now on my knee.

My imagination took a break as I ran out to retrieve the ball, and then back to home plate. Then I repeated the process over and over again.

I was always moving when I was little. Sometimes it was in an organized way, playing the game of the season with friends. Most times it was just me, running and playing the endless day away.

I was still a boy when I began running, but about to make the long journey away from adolescence. It's a pilgrimage most of us can't wait to make. We want independence. We want to be treated like an adult. We yearn to make our mark on the world, and so we go, leaving our childhoods behind us.

Running was a sport in those early years. And while sports and play were largely interchangeable, there was something more serious about my running. I wanted to win races. I yearned to become a champion, and so I pushed myself hard.

Even so, I loved the daily runs. I loved pressing myself in workouts. I loved competing. Running was my recess, my sport, and my freedom.

The other day, I drove through my childhood neighborhood and stopped at the old house to take a look. There was a for-sale sign in the front yard, so just for fun, I used the internet to view pictures of the inside.

I knew it would look different, but I had no idea how much so. There has been some reconstruction. The colors have changed. I barely recognized the place.

It probably wouldn't recognize me either, changed as I am. And yet the bones of the house are the same, as are mine. A part of us will always be the same.

There have been times, in the evolution of life, when I have forgotten that. Life is so different now that I'm older, and the heaviness of responsibility seems to demand all my attention.

And then I run.

Running lets me feel like a boy again, going outside only to move and enjoy myself. I smell the grass, feel the sun and hear the breeze. And even as I run when the breeze is absent, the air still hums in my ears, almost like the world itself is cheering for me.

My days are shorter now. And even as I celebrate the end of every work week, a part of me wonders where all my time is going. Maybe you feel the same way.

If we're not careful, we can take this life, and ourselves, too seriously. I know responsibility is demanding, but that makes my point all the more important.

Childhood, once gone, is gone forever. But the child in you still lives. Let him be joyful.

The Baltimore Running Festival is growing. The event features a marathon, a marathon relay, a half-marathon, and a 5,000-meter race. In 2009, more than twenty-thousand runners participated. They came from forty-four countries and all fifty states to run, and I can hear the collective question coming from the minds of all the non-runners who read this – why?

It is a reasonable question. If you include both the male and female divisions of the races, there were only eight champions. Count the other runners who had enough talent and preparation to potentially win, and you could include no more than a hundred runners in the most elite category. So, the thrill of victory can't be the primary motivator.

Running is hard. It involves discomfort. In order to complete one of the races, participants had to train by running many miles, something the average person might not consider appealing.

Afterwards, the runners had little to show for their effort except for a commemorative shirt and a participant's medal.

And yet, they came on their own initiative, without coercion. They spent their own dollars on registration fees and travel. They used public bathrooms and port-a-pots that were not pleasant. They endured the anxiety of waiting and pressed into the crowded starting areas. And then they ran a race. Why?

If you asked them directly, you would get a wide variety of responses. You would talk to doctors, lawyers, teachers, and soldiers. You would hear from some who were retired and others who were unemployed. And, in the diversity of the stories you would find a common theme - something was missing from each life before running entered into it.

Understanding that leads me to a more important question. We lead lives of abundance. We have conveniences that our parents never dreamed about. There are programs and initiatives designed to provide for the basic needs of every individual, and yet there seems to be more discontent now than ever before. Why?

I'm certain that a heated debate could stem from our attempt to find an answer, but since I'm a simple man, my thinking tends to be simple as well. You won't find anything profound in my conclusion, but here it is anyway.

The answer to both questions is the same. More food, bigger homes, and better gadgets only touch the surface, and one basic human need runs deeper. We need to be fulfilled.

Perhaps you've been wondering yourself – how is it that life can be so full yet so empty as well? It's because fulfillment isn't found in things but in knowing that we can accomplish something significant on our own initiative. And on the streets of Baltimore, twenty-thousand people did just that.

Of course, you don't need running to find fulfillment, but you do need something similar. And if you're not sure what that is for you personally, it might be time to start searching.

The lake was as smooth as a sheet of glass except for a few ripples out near the middle, fish playing near the surface. A turtle poked his head out of the water and then ducked back under as we ran past.

We were running easy and relaxed, soothed by the surroundings. The night before, we had planned on getting up early and we were glad we did. It was a beautiful morning. And best of all, I was running with my daughter again.

We had both taken a long break from running - each of us for different reasons. My reason was simple; chronic injuries made me understand that my only ally was rest.

Her reason was more complex; running itself had become complicated. After breaking into high-school distance running with huge success, it had later been difficult for her to live up to her own expectations. The harder she tried, the harder it seemed. Disappointment mounted, and the pleasure was gone.

It was a challenging time for both of us, but we had each come to our own, similar conclusion: to hold on to something we loved, we had to let it go for a while.

There was some irony in knowing that we had both left and then come back to running at the same time. I hadn't even thought about that until she mentioned it one day. And suddenly, we were partners embarking on a journey to discover what running would mean as we brought it back into our lives.

We turned away from the lake and ran up to a gravel road that stayed near the water. Our run had found a rhythm, and the motion relaxed us. Tall trees gave us shade and created a tunnel as we passed through.

She talked about recent experiences, her plans and her dreams. I listened, remembered how running together had always given me the chance to glance into her life.

The run was over too soon, and afterwards we stretched together and talked a little more. As I watched her, I found myself already looking forward to the next time she would join me for a run.

Yet, in some larger sense, I'm always running beside her, even while we're apart. I know every parent will understand when I say that my emotions are forever linked with hers. Sometimes, it feels like my heart beats in her chest. So, as she begins a new running journey, I find myself making one simple wish – let it bring her joy.

I know she has the same hope for me, and as we both run through the good days and the bad, we'll rely on each other for support and inspiration. She'll ask me lots of questions, and sometimes I'll be helpful.

And, as often as we can, we'll meet and run. We'll talk a bit about our challenges and successes, but none of that will matter very much, as together we find a rhythm and enjoy time with the best running buddy either one of us has ever had.

CHAPTER 13:

GRATITUDE

BEING THANKFUL

———————————•——•———————————

I'm sitting in my running room, a place in the house where I can do my writing and coaching work, and I'm looking at a small wooden box with an inscription on a brass plate entitled "Mil's Money." To most, it probably seems out of place amongst the running memorabilia, even with the medals draped around it.

"Mil" is short for Mildred, my grandmother. When she died in 1993, I offered to say a few words at her funeral. My gesture was declined. We have a big family, and it didn't seem fair to allow one of the grandchildren to speak without the others having the chance to do so.

On the day of the service, I took a run along a familiar back road, thinking about what I would say if I had the opportunity. The winter chill, clinging to the early March air, was more aligned with my mood than the buds and birds that told of spring.

I came upon an old family cemetery and felt an urge to stop there. I walked along the edge reading the names and dates. Surely, some of them had been grandmothers. What words were spoken when they were laid to rest?

As I finished my run, I thought about some of my favorite memories of her, and that's when it came to me. My grandmother and I were connected in a way I hadn't considered before.

When I was growing up, my grandparents and my parents would get together regularly for a game of cards. I can remember going to the kitchen during their games and inquiring as to who was winning. Many times, it was my grandmother who answered, "It doesn't matter who's winning, Dave. We're just having fun." Her factitious tone couldn't mask her competitive nature. She didn't like to lose.

When I arrived for the funeral, my uncle asked if I was still willing to speak, and I had the opportunity to share my thoughts after all. I told the story I just told you, and then a story about myself straining to win in the final meters of a race. My own competitive spirit, I told those gathered, was a gift from her.

In the days that followed, the wooden box was given to me by a friend of my grandmother who had been touched by my words. He had played cards with her on many occasions, and the box was something my grandfather had made for him to keep the quarters that were earned by the winner of each game. His box was so small, he told me, because seldom did he win.

I wish I had recognized her gift before she was gone. Without it, running could never have taken me so far. Still, I'm thankful now to understand that I, too, will pass something along. We all will, and for better or worse, it may live on for generations after we're gone. That's why what we acquire is trivial when compared to what we give away, and why a small wooden box will always hold a place of honor in my running room.

I paced in front of the starting line knowing that I was about to run the most important race of my high school career. As I moved to the line, I looked at the runner in lane one, a reigning state champion. We settled onto the line, the gun fired, and I was on his shoulder.

We were racing a mile, four laps around the track, on a warm, windless day in May. By the time we hit the backstretch, we had already separated ourselves from the rest of the field.

The first lap ended with the starter holding three fingers into the air, but it didn't matter how far we had to go. I was focused on staying just off the lead. I don't remember much about the middle laps except that I became aware that the entire stadium had stopped to watch. No one was throwing or jumping.

When we entered the final turn, I was still on his shoulder. By this time, he knew exactly what I planned to do, and he made his move earlier than I expected. He had pulled ahead by the time we came off the turn.

When I remember the final straight, I relive it in slow motion. I was wide open, straining to catch up. The roar as we passed in front of the crowd helped me maintain my sprint, and we were stride for stride with twenty yards to go. I felt it when he broke, and my momentum carried me across the line a half a stride ahead.

I lingered near the finish line congratulating my competitors, and then I moved toward the infield where I had changed into my racing flats and left a t-shirt behind. As I moved in front of the crowded stands, I heard a voice call out above the others, "Good job, Dave. Well done." It was the voice of my father.

We all need fans, people who stand up and cheer when we win and stand by us when we lose. Maybe I didn't really understand it then, but the most wonderful thing about that moment was finding the faces of my parents in the stands and sharing it with them.

Like most of us, I had to become a father myself to appreciate my own parents. Now I know how deep my feelings go. I've learned how much I'm willing to sacrifice for someone else. And, I've come to understand how much they sacrificed for me.

I can't fully explain the impact that running has had on my life since then. I could never be as productive, content, or balanced if not for running.

And yet, as I watched my parents live into old age, I finally understood that I would never have been as successful, in running or in life, without my greatest fans.

It's impossible to surrender the debt I owe except to return it to my own kids, and I've tried to do that. Still, I want my parents to know that they have fans too. So today, let them hear a voice calling out over the dim roar of life - my voice saying "Good job, Mom and Dad. Well done."

There was a big green tub in my basement that held my old running awards, pictures and newspaper clippings. You might think that I loved going through that stuff, but if you want to know the truth, it was always a mixed blessing.

Inside, there were mementos from some of my best moments - gold medals and finish line celebrations. Then, there were other things that might have seemed just as wonderful if you haven't lived the rest of the story.

There was this one bronze medal in the box, big and shiny with an impressive engraving of a runner, but it's wasn't the medal I wanted. I had trained for months to win that race, but I lost my focus on race day. So, among all the best memories, there are things that remind me of times I could have done better.

A few years ago, I opened the tub and one by one, remembered the day that was connected to each item. On one side of me I placed those things that made me proud. On the other side, I put the ones that made me feel regretful. When I was finished, I gathered up all the disappointments and finally, after all these years, let them go.

In the days that followed I polished my proudest awards and framed my favorite pictures. There's one newspaper picture from my first high school cross-country season. I'm running at practice and staring at the camera with this goofy smile on my face. The floppy left arm will confirm that it's me.

I placed that picture at the doorway of my running room. Then, using the ledge that surrounds the room, I arranged everything until I was happy with the presentation. When I was done, I stood back and admired it all. For the first time in my life, I appreciated my entire running journey, with no conditions attached.

Don't misunderstand. I know the lost opportunities and poor performances are still inside me, but I'm not going to dwell on them anymore. Instead, I'll simply tuck them away for the times when I need inspiration to achieve, or for days when I need wisdom to avoid a mistake.

We all have a pile of stuff to sort through. Maybe yours is in a box in the basement, just like mine was. Maybe it's tucked away in some closet or hidden deep inside your heart. Go through it. Separate out the disappointments. Feel them one last time, and then leave them behind you. You don't need to keep them anymore.

We know how fast time moves along, and yet we spend so much of it lingering in the past. We fool ourselves into thinking that we can somehow recapture a moment, a day, or a year that's gone forever.

We all need to find peace and feel hope, but those things are elusive, until you stop yourself from wondering what could have been and begin dreaming about what might be.

CHAPTER 14:

WONDER

FILLED WITH AWE AND CURIOSITY

It started as a challenge between friends.

Art was one of our training partners, but he was also an excellent cyclist. The rest of us were hard-core runners, and we didn't give Art much respect for his cycling. In fact, we teased him constantly.

Art competed in a 105-mile bike race each year that covered the back roads between Kent Island and Ocean City, Maryland, and our challenge to him was simple. Three of us - Jim, Frank and I - would cover the same 105-mile course by running it as a relay team. Since we didn't have wheels, we would begin running at midnight, five hours before the start of the bike race. Whoever got to Ocean City first would win bragging rights. Art accepted.

When the night of the challenge finally came, I remember standing in the midnight darkness as Art kept us honest about our starting time. Frank took the first leg, and Jim and I climbed into the van that would transport the two of us who weren't running at any given time.

I ran second, and I stood on the side of the road waiting for Frank to touch my hand. Then, I was running down an old, back road in what seemed like the middle of nowhere. My heart raced as I watched the van pull away, the taillights disappearing behind a faraway turn, and I was alone.

I don't ever remember feeling more excitement on a run. I was moving fast, pushed forward by exhilaration. It was pitch-black, and I couldn't help wondering what was watching from the fields surrounding me.

We took turns through the night, and we had over fifty miles behind us by the time we knew Art was getting started.

The road slowly became more visible as the sun rose, but the air warmed quickly. By early morning, we were running in muggy, summer heat, and at a time when water was kept in a jug, not in little bottles, it was the beginning of the end when our water was suddenly lost.

I can't remember exactly how far we had gone when it was my turn to run and I couldn't go. I took a stride, and dehydration caused me to double over with cramps. After a short discussion, we decided we had to stop.

We waited for Art to ride by. He was struggling but got a boost when he saw us. He earned those bragging rights, and I guess we deserved the ribbing that came with it.

We talked for a while about a rematch, but life took its turns, just like it always does, and there never was another challenge.

From time to time, I remember a day I wish I could live over again. Sometimes, it's because I'd like to bring back the pleasure of an experience. Other times, I'd just like another chance to do better. In this case, both apply.

Of course, going back in time is just wishful thinking. So, I'll have to settle for closing my eyes and remembering a long, dark, winding road where running tested my spirit, just like so many other times before and since.

Charlie Ferguson is a runner.

This has always been true. It was true before he ever started running. It would have been true had he chosen never to run a race. It is certainly true now.

It took a while for him to embrace it. He dabbled with youth track and even ran indoor track as a freshman at Westminster High School. But running didn't really click with him, until recently.

He began working harder in spring track, and suddenly Charlie was improving with every race, running a one-mile PR of 5:03.3 in late April. But since he wasn't one of the three fastest milers on the team, he didn't get a chance to run the mile in the championship races, and something inside him felt unfinished.

The five- minute barrier is respected by most milers. Get close, and it doesn't mean much. Get under and, well, it means a lot.

Charlie has a running heritage. I met his grandfather, Dave Kartalia, in the early 1980s, when we both ran in the local races. Dave shared his running passion with his three children, including Anna Ferguson, Charlie's mom; and Steve Kartalia, Charlie's uncle.

Steve, a Westminster High alumnus, still runs at an elite level. He understood Charlie's unfinished business and offered to help.

Steve invited Charlie to join him in a simple affair. They would return to the Westminster High School track, and Steve would try to pace Charlie to a sub-5:00 mile. Since Steve hadn't raced a mile in some time, he wasn't sure he was ready to break 5:00 himself. So, just in case, he invited Ryan Taylor, another Westminster alumnus, who could take over the pacing responsibilities if Steve were to fade.

I learned about the plan when I met my friend, Steve Moore, for a run at Carroll Community College on a Sunday morning in early June. Steve didn't know when the run would happen, but we both agreed it would be fun to watch.

If I have a guardian angel, she must have known that I needed to rediscover the pureness of this sport that I love, because as our run took us onto the Westminster High School track, we found Charlie, Steve, and Ryan warming up there. We joined them.

There were five of us then, moving down the quiet backstretch. In the group were three Westminster High School Owls, and me, a South Carroll Cavalier. Of the three Carroll County, Maryland, graduates, two were previous county mile champions, and the other had come within a second of holding that title. All five of us appreciated the attempt that was about to be made.

As we moved onto the straight that led to the starting line, I saw a small gathering. Charlie's mom, dad, and grandmother were there with cameras to capture the event. Their posture showed anticipation, something you might observe if a loved one was about to race for some prestigious title.

We ran a few more laps before the lucky three decided they were ready.

I walked across the infield to call splits at the two-hundred-meter mark, remembering some of the greatest races I've watched on the Westminster High track. A new one was about to make the list.

I couldn't hear who gave the official start instruction, but I watched the three Owls bolt from the start and quickly form a line as they rounded the first turn. Steve set the pace, Ryan placed himself at the rear to monitor developments, and Charlie ran between them, trusting in his company.

They breezed by me as I called out 37 seconds. The pace was perfect.

They slowed a little on the next 200 meters, finishing the first lap in just over 1:15, but by the time they ran by me at 600 meters, the pace was perfect again. They hit the 800-meter mark at 2:29.

Everyone who's ever raced a mile understands that the outcome is decided on the third lap. The amiable time ends because the body has consumed all the readily available resources. After that, it must seek and find fuel in the places where pain resides.

Steve was edging away when they ran by me at 1000 meters. Charlie's shoulders were pulled up, his stride less fluid.

We could all see Charlie struggle. His mom, dad, and grandmother all reacted just as you would in the same situation, with a combination of worry, hope, and prayerful vibes.

As the third lap ended, Steve was ten meters in front, but Charlie was still on pace. Ryan, who had been waiting for the right moment, ran up beside Charlie and began talking him through the painful strides. They passed me for the last time in 4:29.

The uncertainty ended soon after that, as Charlie accelerated off the final turn and sprinted towards the finish. All the milers who preceded him on that track would have been proud as Charlie crossed the line in 4:58.5, just more than a second behind his honored uncle.

You can imagine the celebration as well as I can describe it – excitement, embracing, handshakes and laughter – all in honor of a broken barrier.

We all have hidden talents, seeds planted throughout our lineage. The uncovering isn't easy; the digging is hard work.

And even when we discover a talent, we may decide not to pursue it, but trust in this: there is great potential inside each one of us. It's up to you to find yours.

The sun was going down by the time I left the house.

It was a Thursday in 1989, three weeks before a target race I was hoping to win, and I needed to run a workout that would tell me the one thing I always wanted to know before a big race - was I ready?

I used the mile and a half run to the local college as a warm-up, and then ran a couple easy laps on the empty, dark track.

I planned to do eight half-mile repeats at just faster than race pace with a short half-lap jog that I would cover in about one minute. I had done the same workout dozens of times before, each time feeling slightly apprehensive beforehand. It was a hard and brutally honest test of my preparedness.

I set my stopwatch to zero, pressed go, and began the first two-lap repeat.

I moved around the turn and away from the blackest side of the track. There was a distant streetlight that shed a soft glow onto the opposite side, causing my own shadow to run up beside me. I could see my legs turning over on the infield as I moved onto the straight.

The first repeat was always one of the hardest. No matter how well I warmed up, it never felt comfortable. I focused on feeling my pace while ignoring the watch, wanting instinct to govern my effort.

The blackness swallowed me again as I rounded the far turn, and I tried to relax as the first lap ended. "One more lap," were the last three words that entered my mind before I drifted into the trance that protected my consciousness from ruinous thought.

Of all the qualities of success in distance running, I'm convinced that the ability to deeply concentrate is one of the most important. A wandering mind looks for trouble, and when you are running hard trouble is easy to find.

I finished the first repeat and eased into my recovery jog. My breathing settled quickly, and as I moved into the soft glow, I checked my watch – 2:32. Good.

The second repeat felt better than the first one. By then, my blood was flowing freely into the needy muscle fibers. The third and fourth repeats were much like the second, and I ran all three in the exact same time as the first one.

The fifth repeat was harder. The weight of the fatigue was starting to grow, and as I moved into the dim light, I glanced over to check my shadow's cadence. "You can do this," I reassured myself.

The repeat ended, and my heaving breath found mercy in the minute of recovery. I lifted my wrist into the light - 2:31.

The sixth repeat dared me to give up, but I absorbed myself in the effort, dismissing the distracting thought. I could feel the deep crevices in my lungs pulled for breath, and I knew they were at their limits.

The repeat ended with another 2:32, and I allowed a short celebration in the half-lap recovery, "Just two more."

The seventh repeat was physically hard, but emotionally lifting. I visualized the final mile of my target race, could see my best competition running beside me, and we kept pace together as I finished the repeat on the dark side of the track.

In the last recovery, my lungs struggled as I jogged around the turn, and hardly settled as I neared the start of the last repeat. But I accelerated as I approached the line, started my watch, and raced around the first turn.

The greatest antidote to discomfort is the knowing it is about to end. I hurt, but I didn't care. I pushed myself hard, and on the last lap I imagined the stadium was full, bright, and cheering as I ran away from my competition.

I crossed the line, staggered to a walk, and then slowly moved into a spot of light to see the watch – 2:30.

I was exhausted but elated on the jog back home.

Two days later, on tired legs, I ran a relatively relaxed 26:40 to win a five-mile race at Hopkins University, and I had the answer to my question – I was ready.

On the morning of my 10K target race, 3,000 runners gathered at the start. I scanned the crowd looking to see who was there and found my best competition. Jim Hage, a three-time Olympic Trials qualifier was there. In prior years, Hage's presence would have been enough to have me thinking of second place, but not that day. Both my mind and my body were ready to race.

The early miles passed just as I had envisioned them. I was tucked into the lead pack feeding off the rhythm of the group. The miles passed quickly, and the pack slowly dissolved. There were just five of us by the time we hit the four-mile mark.

Even after all the months of perfect preparation, a chance is the best you can hope for. I was two miles away from the finish line with a chance to run the best race of my running life.

Then, just after four miles, my concentration broke. It was like having the Novocain wear off too soon, and suddenly my mind shifted away from the task and toward the discomfort. I drifted back from the leaders and ultimately finished in fourth place.

I used to think that I had failed, that the hard work was wasted, but I was wrong.

The habit of setting and pursuing goals is an important one. Soon after that race, my serious racing days ended, but the habit didn't.

There's more. My spirit has a need to be tested. Everyone's does. Try it and see how alive you feel.

There are all kinds of reasons not to try something you want to do, and every reason is real. Fear and apprehension torment everybody, but you can resist those things.

And when you do, when you fight back against the demons that have always beat you in the past, there's no way you can lose.

CHAPTER 15:

ACCEPTANCE
BELIEVING IN GOODNESS

———————————•—————————————

Running isn't all good.

I know that may be a surprise to those who read my stuff. I've shared many worthy stories about how running has enhanced my life and the lives of other people. These have been stories of strength and perseverance, of courage and tenacity, and of hope and peace.

But running isn't all good. There are five drawers in my dresser. Two of them are cluttered with running clothes, meaning the other three are cluttered with all the things a normal person would wear. A runner's wardrobe must be diverse, which brings me to another bad thing.

In Maryland, there are about 30 days a year with weather that's perfect for running, which means about 335 days are less than perfect. Of course, there are various degrees of imperfection, ranging from annoying to unpleasant. And then there are the downright awful days, not fit for man nor beast, but forced upon a runner. If a run is on the schedule, it will be done no matter what is falling from the sky or blowing in our faces.

The one bad thing everyone understands is this – pain. We have lots of it, but the kind non-runners think about doesn't last very long. The heaving discomfort of an unfit body goes away; but runners like to push themselves, and it hurts when we do.

There is stiffness. Our muscles, used to motion, don't like sitting. So, when we rise, the first few steps are troublesome. We do our best to act normal, but inside we know everyone watching is thinking the same thing – how can this guy run when he can't even get out of his chair?

And then there's the unmentionable issues, things we can't talk about with people who don't run.

Inevitably, though we do everything we can to avoid it, we will be miles away from the place we started, and nature will call. Not in the way we all hope it will, with soothing sounds and beautiful landscapes, but in the same way it calls to the guy who ate too much Mexican food. And that guy only has to walk a few steps to get to the bathroom.

In the winter our noses run faster than we do. Wiping is a matter of preference; sleeves and gloves are options. We often miss some, and unknowingly carry the smears around on our cheeks, only to become aware when we see our disagreeable face in the mirror.

In the summer, we smell. It's fine as long as we stay together, but in isolation we stand out. When we wait in the check-out line with our bottle of Gatorade, everyone knows the source of the unpleasant odor. It's us.

I could go on, talking about how hard it is to fit runs into busy schedules, how boring we are when we talk about running, but you get the idea. Running isn't all good.

So why do we do it?

I can't speak for all runners, but on behalf of myself, here's why.

I run because it makes me better, not better than anyone else, but better than I'd be if I didn't run.

I'm calmer. Running sooths my emotions, let's me get rid of the muck that accumulates day-to-day. I think more clearly too, so problems don't linger when I'm running.

I'm more sure of myself. The small, daily accomplishment helps me feel good about myself. When I overcome all the obstacles running presents, I feel capable.

Running reinforces the principles I like to live by. Work ethic, discipline, and perseverance are handy habits.

I know what I'm like when I can't run. I'm better when I can.

Life isn't all good either. I probably don't have to elaborate for you to agree.

But here's the thing – dwell on the challenge and the challenge gets worse. Decide to move yourself forward, and something remarkable happens.

Conditions are never as bad as they seem. Challenge is never insurmountable. What seems impossible isn't.

I know I'm lucky. By many standards, my life is charmed. But I've seen enough hardship to know there's one thing that will never get you past it – cowering.

I don't' mind the weather. I don't care if I end up with a little snot on my cheeks, or if I feel stiff getting up from my chair. I don't even mind the pain, because I know that once I put myself in motion, I can do anything.

So can you.

In the 1980s, Westminster was the home of one of the premier races in Maryland, the Frostbite 5K and 15K. Held the first weekend in January, these races started and finished on the campus of Western Maryland (now McDaniel) College.

Both race courses left the college and then went out and back on Uniontown Road. When you look from a distance at Uniontown Road coming back toward the college, you'll notice that there is a hill that looks like a quarter-mile-high wall. The courses were hard.

Despite that, the race attracted the best runners in the mid-Atlantic area. Names like Doub, Smith, Chattin, Stevens, Kartalia and Simonsick held spots on the top-performance listings.

It was many years ago now, December 1985, that I decided to run the Frostbite 15K on January 5, 1986.

I had had mixed results for much of 1985. I couldn't seem to match many of my race times from the previous year, but things started to come together that fall. In October I ran a 25:43 5-mile PR, and that was enough to re-energize my training.

In the 28 days leading up to Frostbite, I completed 34 runs and workouts totaling 270 miles. Though not high mileage by elite standards, it was a lot for me.

I began the race hoping to run an even pace over the hilly course and settled in around 15th place in the first mile. During the 2nd mile, I began moving up.

I remember coming up beside Mike Spinnler and chatting for a few minutes. Spinnler had recently moved to Westminster and we were quickly becoming good friends. His credentials included a 2:28 marathon and two JFK 50-mile victories, but he was hampered by injury at that point.

I left Spinnler and continued passing runners, finding myself in fourth place after the third mile. That's when Jeff Scuffins came up from behind and settled in next to me.

Scuffins was one of the runners I ran against in high school who would later become national class. The following year, he would run 2:14:01 to win the Marine Corps Marathon, a course record that continues to stand.

I had no business running with Scuffins, but he was there for a workout, and my pace suited him.

The three runners in front of us, John Doub, Chris Chattin and Jeff Smith, were legendary; at least they were to me. In the distance we could see them battling.

We turned around and began heading back. A hill after the five-mile mark rivaled the one near the finish, but I rushed up it and hoped I could recover at the top. I crested the hill feeling strong.

To fully appreciate how I was feeling at this point in the race, you need to have a little insight. I had finished first in a lot of local races. That summer I won the Westminster Road Runners Club summer series for the fourth straight year. That didn't satisfy me.

I dreamed about reaching the next level, but in big races like this one, I was typically struggling to finish in the top ten. So, even if Scuffins was slacking, it was special for me to be six miles in to a 15k race with him on my shoulder and three elite runners still in sight.

And then Jeff Smith, the 1982 Marine Corp Marathon champion, started falling back.

Scuffins began to encourage me. I pushed harder.

I ran the rest of the race thinking I could catch Smith. If he was struggling, I figured, the final hill would finish him. It didn't. When I turned into the college, Scuffins still by my side, Smith was too far ahead.

As we approached the finish line, Scuffins gestured for me to move in front, and I was more than happy to oblige him. The official results listed the top five finishers this way – Doub, Chattin, Smith, Griffin, Scuffins. I was happy to be on that list.

In the weeks following the race, I got a picture in the mail from Scuffins showing the two of us nearing the finish line. "To Dave," a note on the back of the picture said, "You got lucky. It will never happen again."

Frostbite turned out to be the highlight of my year. By spring, I was dealing with a knee injury that was later diagnosed as a cartilage tear. Surgery techniques weren't as advanced as they are today, and I spent most of the year recovering.

I returned to top shape by late 1987, and over the next few years ran some of my best races, but I can't say I ever felt closer to the elite than at Frostbite 1986.

After so many years, there are times when it begins to feel like my fastest races never happened. Athletic achievement doesn't age particularly well.

I guess we've all lost something we'd like to have back. The emotion is real. It's right to allow yourself to feel it, but when you're ready, it's also important to understand something else.

Nothing, and no one, is gone that has shaped you. This day can be a perfect combination of all the good things in your past and all the great dreams for your future. Let yourself be grateful.

The leaves remaining on the trees were brittle and brown, waiting only for the next hard breeze to blow before falling. Most trees were bare, already fully surrendered to the short, cold November days.

The calendar said there were still three weeks of autumn left, but late fall is winter's twin.

I had woken up with nothing planned on a vacation day that would be lost if not taken. When I was younger, I may have let it go, but time is too precious to me now.

I drove to my favorite running place, got out of the car, and did some active isolated stretching. Then I spent a few moments standing in the cold, deciding whether or not to shed my running tights. I took them off.

I left my car behind with a slow forward shuffle, typical now for the first few moments of a run. I left the road in favor of a dirt trail, traveled more on horseback than foot, and I was alone. I don't tolerate the cold as well as I once did, but I do love the isolation it brings.

The bare trees lining the pathway were still. I wondered if they knew I was passing, and if so, did they remember me from the last time. I smiled at myself; the most interesting notions enter my brain while I'm running.

I've been recovering from a calf strain, and most of my recent runs had been short and timid. I was prepared for the calf to nag me, but it didn't, and it felt good to move along without concern.

There were no clouds to block the sunshine, so every beam reached the earth, making everything seem happy. Even the grass, once defeated by the morning frost, rose just enough to feel the warmth.

I felt it too, and I was glad I left my tights in the car.

I'm not training for anything in particular. Running used to require a purpose, some driving motivation to keep me going. But for now, it's become a welcomed escape, releasing me from the pressing responsibilities that sometimes rule my life.

I ran as far as the dirt trail would take me, and then found an old country road to explore. I climbed a long hill that winded me, but otherwise ran along feeling more comfortable than when I'm slouching in a chair.

Seasons begin and end on their own whim, at least that's how it seems to me. Sometimes it's a gentle transition. Sometimes it's a jolting change.

How I feel about the weather has more to do with perception than anything else. A 40-degree day in November feels cold, but the exact same day in February seems perfect.

Life is the same way. A child may think I'm old. My father says I'm young. Some people think I'm fast, but when I compare my younger and older selves, I feel slow.

We all view the world through our own eyes. Each day has been scripted by all the days that preceded it. Our awareness equals the sum of our experience.

Since I chose this running life, I've been defeated and victorious. I've run through miles in weakness and in strength. I've started and finished runs in all kinds of moods and run in every imaginable type of weather.

Running showed me that even bitter air can become beautiful if you're willing to immerse yourself in it.

If you've never run, you probably think fatigue grows with every passing mile, but that's not how it is for me. As I ran on that old road, I felt completely free.

I found a grass trail that led me where I wanted to go, and I left the road to cross it. My flying feet landed on the barren ground, reshaping it, and me, if only in the smallest way.

I reached my car and stopped, and then I stood for a while, looking at the surrounding fields and hillsides. Everything knew as well as I did, the hard freeze will be here soon.

I can't wait to run through it.

CHAPTER 16:

REVERENCE
BELIEVING IN GOODNESS

———————◆ ▶———————

When I was in high school, the South Carroll Invitational was the largest cross-country meet of the season. Teams from three states gathered on our home course.

At the end of the school day, I simply walked down to the locker room, got dressed, and stepped into a fall running festival.

Earlier in the day, my teachers didn't know I wasn't paying attention in class. My nerves wouldn't let me think about anything other than the meet.

I've always loved the color of sports, and when I stepped outside, it was fun seeing the abundance of color moving around the school grounds. Our team gathered at a corner of the building and watched with fascination.

Our coach was distracted with the workings of the meet, so we were pretty much left to ourselves. We warmed up in a cluster, trying our best to calm one another.

We jogged past the starting line. A new stadium, not so new anymore, stands over the spot now. But back then, the area behind the school was vacant ground, except for the baseball field, which was exactly where it is today.

Before all three of the South Carroll Invitational races I ran, I had glorious dreams. I imagined I would have a break-out race, cheered on by a loyal crowd. I saw myself running with the leaders, far ahead of runners who usually beat me.

At the start, there was a short downhill section, so the race began with a stampede. Most high school runners start too fast, and I wasn't any smarter than the others. I surged from the beginning, until my body reminded me it was a three-mile race.

We ran in a circle behind the school before running two long loops around a large cornfield. Each loop began with a hard climb, followed by a stretch of gradual decent. By my senior year, I knew every square foot of ground we passed over.

The dreams I had before each race never really came true, but I was beginning to think big, and that always precedes the actual doing.

Whenever I'm in the area these days, I try to stop by South Carroll High School. I park my car and walk around.

When I'm there, it still feels like 1978. Every detail is familiar.

I start by walking a lap around the track, remembering where our team would cluster during meets. I relive races in my mind.

When I leave the track, I walk behind the school, thinking about conversations I had and the people I had them with. I remember a black brick that seems out of place among all the red ones, and I remember looking out of a classroom window and wondering how it go there.

When I walk the old cross-country course, I smell the same smells, feel the touch of the same breeze and hear the rustling of the same trees.

It's hard for me to comprehend the time that's gone by. I know how long ago it was, and yet something in my heart makes it feel like yesterday.

There are times when I'm afraid I'll forget what happened there. My walks give me the chance to reclaim the memories and memorialize the place where my running journey started.

If you've read this far, you already know where the journey led me. My values, my capability and my passion are all byproducts of my running.

After being around the sport for so long, I've watched hundreds of new runners. Many have been a part of my Flying Feet program as well. Almost without exception, no one understands the depth of personal growth running can bring them.

But anyone who persists with running learns soon enough, our sport changes people. That's why we hold running, and our fellow runners, in such high esteem, and why I'll keep returning to South Carroll High School to pay homage to my earliest memories.

The gun sounded, and Mike Konsen sprinted with the pack.

Mike was a year ahead of me at South Carroll High School, a senior who ran track for the first time as a junior. He quickly earned a place on our two-mile relay team, and just as quickly became my closest friend. He had an old VW Beetle, and we used it to traverse our tiny universe.

We were running the opening race of a 1978 outdoor track meet, and Mike positioned us near the lead before handing the baton to John Horton.

John was a fast sophomore, and one of the funniest people I've ever known. His antics were often the highlight of my day, but he was also a profound thinker.

We had deep conversations about the lives we were living and the people we were living them with. After a time of serious discussion, John would end with a joke, and we'd return to our quirky teenage selves.

John was strong, the only guy I've ever known who could walk around on his hands. He barreled toward me on the track, and I grabbed the baton and sprinted onto the shoulder of the guy just in front.

Our team was in third place at that point. The leader was already half way around the first turn.

Todd Ashley, another sophomore, would run our anchor leg. Todd was the most talented of our group, already one of the best runners in the state.

My motivation to perform was never higher than it was when I was on a relay team. I wasn't running for myself; I was running for them. As I neared the end of the first lap, I could see the three of them lining the track. I passed them, hearing their encouraging shouts.

And it wasn't just about the race. If I had collapsed on the track in front of them, they would have surrounded me, protected me, done whatever it was I needed them to do.

I managed to move into second place on the final straight, but I had made up little ground on the leader. I lunged forward as I gave Todd the baton, and then gasped to the side of the track.

Mike, John, and I, each one of us in different stages of recovery, watched as Todd began to gain ground on the leader. By the time he came by us, he had made up half the distance and showed no sign of slowing. We cheered as he whizzed by.

Coming off the final turn, Todd approached the leader and they came down the straight sprinting next to one another. Todd hit the tape just in front, and we all gathered together to celebrate what was then the fastest two-mile relay time in the school's history.

A couple years ago, when I heard Glenn Frey of the Eagles passed away, I was instantly back in high school. Something about music can return us to the days when we first listened to it.

More times than not, the Eagles played in Mike Konsen's VW as we drove to and from the places we would go.

The songs were perfect, not as hard as heavy metal, but with a fierce and compelling lyric. We heard anger, confusion and passion, and we swore the band knew just what we were thinking.

I ran hundreds of miles with an Eagles song in my head, telling me to "Take it Easy" sometimes and "Take it to the Limit" others. There was wisdom in the messages, and the melodies became life-long companions.

I've only run on one formal relay team since high school, and it was a 3-person marathon. I ran the first leg, a half-marathon, and then tapped hands with Jim Shank who ran the second leg. Jim had become my closest running friend after high school.

Todd Ashley ran the anchor leg for us that day. I still have the silver plate the three of us won together.

Our closest companions always stay with us, no matter whether they're in or out of our lives at this particular moment. If any one of those guys handed me the baton today, I'd still run my heart out for them.

I needed their companionship when I was young. And when no friends were around, I'd turn on my music, and find a voice who understood what I was feeling.

I saw the Eagles in concert a few times over the years, and it makes me sad to think I'll never see the full band again. Their songs were with me when I was nothing more than a confused kid, and they've been with me ever since.

I guess there's a chance I'll never see my old friends again either. Life has pulled us away from one another. But as long as my mind holds memories and my heart feels passion, they'll stay with me too.

My footsteps created an echo in the empty house. It was the day after we moved away from our home of 20 years, and I had come to make sure we didn't leave anything behind.

I went from room to room, double checking the emptiness. Dust bunnies scattered here and there as I walked by. Other than that, there was nothing left; we had moved everything.

My task complete, I walked around a second time. I stood in the rooms of my daughter and son, remembering their youngest days. I could see them sleeping, butt pointed to the ceiling, in their toddler beds.

I remembered the parties, Christmastimes, and places where baskets were hidden on Easter morning. The years raced through my memory; I was taking an inventory of the life we lived there.

Standing on the back deck, I remembered watching my son walk across the yard towards me. He grabbed me as hard as he ever has, before or since, and sobbed. My children's heartbreak has always left me feeling helpless; all I could do was hug him back.

When I was ready to leave the house, I stood inside the front door paralyzed by the permanence of my next step. Then I gathered myself together and locked the door behind me.

A few days later, I met my Flying Feet group for our last workout of the season. I stood in front of them, scanning down the line of faces looking back at me.

Some of them had accomplished remarkable things.

One runner had a long-standing goal to finish a half marathon in less than two hours. All the other attempts had ended with frustration, but not this one. He finished the Hershey Half Marathon with time to spare, and with a greater appreciation of his own capability.

But there were others who weren't so happy. Despite great discipline and determination, race day ended with an unfulfilled goal.

So before sending my runners off for a final workout, I looked into the eyes of the contented and the unsatisfied.

Pick something, anything about life, and you'll realize that it is some combination of good and bad. The food you most enjoy is unhealthy. The luxuries you want cost too much. Dreams inspire and, at times, disappoint.

After each training cycle, there is a time of rest and recovery for my running group. They take time off to refresh themselves physically and emotionally before starting the next training cycle.

Many of them resist it, caught on the notion that a break might leave them weaker. But taking time for renewal is a cleansing habit; it helps you decide what to carry forward and what to leave behind.

After we depart, we arrive.

Every day, every run, has intrinsic value. Only your own misgivings can take that away. But misgivings are a burden from the past, and that's where you should leave them.

Only then can you lock the door behind you and make the most of whatever comes next

CHAPTER 17:

AUTHENTICITY

TRUE TO ONE'S CHARACTER AND SPIRIT

When I was growing up on Carroll Highlands Road, my home was warm and safe. I was free to explore the yards nearby, and I would venture away for hours.

A few doors down, I'd stop on the front lawn to visit the dog, and the woman who lived there, I've long since forgotten her name, would come out to talk. She welcomed me and helped me feel cared for.

She wasn't good at predicting the future though. She'd tell me I was going to grow tall because my knees were a long way away from my feet.

Everything about Carroll Highlands Road was comforting, and I loved being there.

My comfort level declined immediately when the school bus picked me up. I didn't always know where to sit. Kids could be unruly.

The anxiousness peppered most of my school years. I wanted to assert myself, to be strong, but I don't remember finding the courage to do that very many times.

The change happened when I started running. It didn't occur all at once, but I slowly became assured. I discovered my competitive spirit and a way to use it.

By the time I was a high school senior, I had an identity, and a place away from home where I felt good about myself, and then I lost it.

I didn't really know what to do after I graduated from high school, and I don't remember having anyone to explain my choices. I ended up enrolling at Frederick Community College, a school without a cross-country team. I had to balance school with work, and for some reason I just wasn't prepared.

I quit college before the end of the semester.

I got a job that I didn't like. With a little help from my grandmother, I bought a mobile home, and I settled in to an unsatisfying routine. My isolated runs helped me stay sane.

I don't know how I heard about it, but the local running club, The Westminster Road Runners, held a race that fall. It was the club championship 10K. I went.

The race began at the end of a farmhouse driveway on Lemmon Road. Less than a hundred runners, none of whom I recognized, gathered there for the instructions.

When the race started I settled into a small group of runners behind Dave Pabst, who gradually pulled away from us. Pabst wasn't too far ahead by the time we reached the two-mile mark, and I decided to surge and come up on his shoulder.

I had run a handful of road races before this one, but those were mostly for fun with my high school teammates. This was the first time I had entered to race seriously. My inexperience showed.

The effort I'd expended to catch up caused me to fall back again. I slowed until I recovered, and then I made another surge. By the time we reached five miles, I had fallen back and surged to catch Pabst's several times.

The final mile was on Sullivan Road. I had fallen back again as Lemmon Road appeared, and I knew we were getting close to the finish. I surged one last time to get on Pabst's shoulder.

We hit Lemmon Road together. The race finished on the farmhouse driveway, and we sprinted up the gravel.

Everything in my being wanted to win. I wanted to assert myself. I wanted to feel secure that I could fight when I needed to.

The award ceremony was modest. They gave Dave Pabst his first-place trophy, and I waited to see what my second-place award would be. When my name was called, I received a club t-shirt, and immediately decided that I'd be back the following year for the trophy.

Now, over the course of more than forty years, I've competed in hundreds of races. I'll keep competing too, because I never feel more satisfied than I do after I've tried my best in an honest race.

I had lunch with a friend the other day. We're both aging distance runners, and we reminisced about how lucky we've been to have running as an outlet for our competitive nature.

We talked about how most everyone has some competitive instinct. It's innate; hundreds of years ago you couldn't survive without it. But not everyone is lucky enough to have an outlet, and it can be used in ways that lead to self-destruction.

We compete for status. We compete for titles. We use the things we own as a basis for comparison.

It's healthy to have dreams, and it's right to work hard to get what you want in life. But thousands of people will lose their virtue as they compete for wealth, and powerful people seldom show real compassion.

If you had to choose, would you rather love what you have or love who you are?

You'll never have everything you want and trying to get it will lead your life into a never-ending spiral. I can't say that it's easier to become the person you want to be, but it is less complicated.

Start by naming the qualities you most value, and then find an outlet to begin crafting those qualities into yourself. Then, even small gains will feed your passion. And values, not things, will define your life.

I have written a running column since 2006. In the years I was writing, I did little more than put my thoughts and feelings on paper.

As much as I've shared my stories with you, I've had the chance to ponder what my running experiences have taught me, and the process has been life-changing.

I didn't begin running with a purposeful plan. It was more happenstance than a decision that led me to it. And it wasn't until my fastest running was well behind me that I understood how running shaped my life.

Writing has helped me capture and describe the value in what some might call a simple pastime.

But now, after more than 300 columns and two books, the words aren't coming as easily, and I've decided to take a break from writing for a while.

Stepping away from something can mean you never have a chance to come back. So, if these become parting words, I'd like to share what I most value from this running life of mine.

I value simplicity. Life's too hard to put on airs. Being myself is easy and running helped me realize that there's never a need to be anything else.

I value effort. Giving up and backing down never lead to good things. Running taught me that fatigue is relative. I can be exhausted and still find strength.

I value solitude. I can be alone and not lonely, and it's hard to imagine a life when that won't come in handy.

No matter how gifted you are, or how fortunate, you'll never find real success until you accept responsibility for yourself. Running makes that point perfectly clear.

No one can make you take a first step. Only your own ambition can move you in a chosen direction. And once you're in motion, it is only internal fortitude that will keep you moving forward.

No one else can push you over a hill. You alone will need to endure the difficult miles.

Some will tell you that it's easier to assign responsibility to your circumstances, that your success is somehow linked to things outside of your control, but that is a crippling message. Until you believe that your situation is a reflection of your own actions and choices, you can never choose to change your situation.

Running helped me find joy in my boyhood, and it still awakens the boy in me today. It led me to understand how thrilling it can be to dream big and then move towards those dreams under my own power. Running taught me how to deal with adversity. It led me to believe that strength is cultivated in struggle.

Because I've accepted the challenges running presents, I know that I can also face the challenges of life. Confidence, once acquired, can be used in many ways.

As I've gotten older, running has been a means of finding peace. I can settle ailing emotions. I can resolve my own disputes. The noise of life quiets when I'm in motion.

And as I've learned to deal with my aging body, running has taught me that I'm most happy when I am gracious, when I realize that, above all, I am blessed.

It's important to define yourself. Just as I've done here, you should be able to describe the things you value. Make a list and live with it for a few days. Once it feels right, keep those values in mind as you live day-to-day.

Living a life in harmony with your values is the only lasting pathway to happiness.

Then, when life steers you away from who you want to be, you will have a compass, formed through you own conscious.

That, more than anything, will keep you running in your chosen direction.

ABOUT THE AUTHOR

Dave Griffin began running in 1976 as a high school freshman. He ran competitively through 1989 with PRs that include a 25:43 5M, a 32:11 10K and a 1:12:24 half marathon. In 1986, much of the medial meniscus was removed during surgery to repair a non-running injury. The doctor advised Dave to stop running, warning that he would get arthritis if he continued. He returned to running and racing after the surgery, running some of his best races in 1987-89.

After a 12-year period of casual running when his children were young, he returned to competitive running as a master.

The doctor's warning came true in 2005, when Dave developed arthritis in his right knee. The years since have been riddled with injury, including a stress fracture in his right medial condyle while training for the 2012 Boston Marathon.

Dave started the Flying Feet Running Programs in 2004 while his daughter, Katie, was running in high school. The program has since grown to provide year-round coaching and support to runners of all experience and talent levels in the Carroll County, Maryland, area.

Dave began writing about running and life in 2006, when his bi-weekly column, Dave Griffin on Running, was introduced. His book, In the Distance – Why we struggle through the demands of running and how it leads us to peace, was published in 2015.

You can find Dave on the internet at www.flyingfeetrunning.com and on Facebook by searching for After the Last PR.

Made in the USA
Columbia, SC
11 December 2018